The Long Yearning's End
Stories of Sacrament and Incarnation

Patrick Hannon, CSC

PUBLICATIONS

DEDICATION

To Fitz, my friend

THE LONG YEARNING'S END
Stories of Sacrament and Incarnation
by Patrick Hannon, CSC

Edited by Gregory F. Augustine Pierce
Cover design by Tom A. Wright
Text design and typesetting by Patricia A. Lynch

"The Banjo Man" was first published in *Diamond Presence: Twelve Stories of Finding of God at the Old Ball Park* (ACTA Publications, 2004).

Scripture quotations are from the *New Revised Standard Version Bible*, copyright © 1989 by the Division of Christian Education of the National Council of the Churches of Christ in the USA. Used by permission.

Published by ACTA Publications, 5559 W. Howard Street, Skokie, IL 60077-2621, (800) 397-2282, www.actapublications.com

Library of Congress Catalog number: 2009930508
Hardcover ISBN: 978-0-87946-402-8
Softcover ISBN: 978-0-87946-403-5

Printed in Canada by Graphics TwoFortyFour, Inc.

Year 20 19 18 17 16 15 14 13 12 11 10 09
Printing 15 14 13 12 11 10 9 8 7 6 5 4 3 2 First

♻ Text is printed on 100% post-consumer waste recycled paper.

CONTENTS

Sunrise, Sunset

D ad died on a Wednesday. By Friday dusk my brothers and I were traipsing along the short fairways of the Indian Camp Golf Course in Tulelake, California, where our dad had played often after he retired from lawyering and moved back to his boyhood home. "The First Annual William Hannon Memorial Golf Tournament" we were to call it, and anytime my brothers and I hit the links now, we relive the day we first golfed in Dad's honor. That Friday evening, though, we went golfing because we were anxious with grief and needed to do something, anything, to distract us.

Mom, Grandma, and my sisters had stayed at the farmhouse. Music was blaring from the living room as I climbed onto the bed of the pickup to leave for the golf course. My sisters were in prime form, singing mostly in tune, and though I can't say for sure, I bet they were dancing.

We boys arrived at the golf course around five in the late afternoon. The sun was teetering on the edge of the hills to the west. It appeared to me to be worn and weary, like a working stiff ready to punch the clock after a long shift. A cool breeze kept the mosquitoes at bay, and the air smelled of wheat and barley and harvested potatoes. There also seemed to be the lingering aroma of musk that denoted my father's presence. Earlier that day I had found my dad's flannel jacket hanging on a hook near the washing machine. I buried my face in it and inhaled deeply, breathing in my father. Everything around me carried with it hints of Dad's presence, especially my brother's faces: the same grin and grimace, the same jaw line and crow's feet. My father's ghost happily haunted Indian Camp that Friday.

The first fairway faces west. It's a par-3, two hundred yards, give or take, from tee to hole. Greg was the first to go, and he set the tone by slicing the ball deep into the rocky rough to the right. His swing is a sight to behold, wrong for a hundred reasons but earnest and heartfelt. Cashing in the one and only mulligan we normally allowed one another for the day, Greg went at it again, this time whacking the ball to within fifteen feet of the hole. He strutted down the fairway with the rest of us in tow. So began one of the most joyful nights of my life.

❋ ❋ ❋ ❋ ❋ ❋ ❋

My brothers may dispute my recollection, but we were awful golfers that day. We swung our clubs like peasants with scythes in hand, hacking and slashing at the ball. We were the Keystone Kops in blue jeans, running this way and that, cussing and spitting and granting mulligans to each other like this was our last day on the planet. Apparently, we had all unconsciously decided to honor our father by playing exactly as he would have.

By the third hole, Brian suggested that one of us run down to the market across the street from the course and buy a couple of six-packs of beer. One of us did, and we took our time with each hole, sipping our beers, resting our arms on each other's shoulders, reminiscing about Dad, and searching for errant balls. We walked the course as if we were making our way to an important destination, our own Calvary, unhurried and purposeful. Every moment was ripe with significance; every word spoken was meaningful.

By the sixth hole it was clear to all of us that we hadn't sufficient sunlight to finish the course, so we decided to make our way to the ninth hole and sit by the empty pond and finish our beers. The sun was nearly set and the sky was burnt orange and red, reclining on a bed of purple. The dying sun's last blessing, Grandma used to call it.

The early evening coaxed out of us stories of our father, and we listened to them with heedful reverence. We had become caretakers of the tradition, keepers of the story. We belly-laughed and wept, sometimes at the same time, for our father had odd penchants and exasperating habits, all of them endearing. A man of ironclad memory, Dad would inexplicably forget our names when we brought our girlfriends home for supper. Every evening after dinner, in front of Walter Cronkite, he would at the appointed time let out a prodigious burp and then sit back in his easy chair with adolescent satisfaction as one of his brood who happened to be downwind let out a painful groan. We could set our watches to his belching. Coming home late from an evening out with the Missus, he would, against the vehement protestations of said Missus, proceed to wake his children and rile us all up. We would then wrestle and spar with one another long into the night and early morning, while Dad went to bed and slept like a baby.

By the time we left the golf course that evening, our sides ached from the laughter borne of a hundred memories of a man we all loved and already missed terribly.

I remember thinking that evening that I had never felt closer to my brothers in my life. I loved them thoroughly and was stunned by the realization that it was suffering and grief that had brought me to this moment of grace, this experience of God. I willingly walked the road to Calvary that Jesus walked, because in the end I was left with cavernous, consequential joy. It was a sunset's blessing. It made my grief bearable.

❀ ❀ ❀ ❀ ❀ ❀ ❀

I was up early the next morning just before dawn. The night before, my brothers and I returned to the farmhouse to find the womenfolk, well, living it up. They were tipsy, so they were all gangly arms and wet lips, hugging us and kissing us as if we had just returned from the war. It was all a bit unconventional; the farmhouse that night certainly lacked the heavy somberness usually reserved for such occasions, but we welcomed that sad joy. Watching my eighty-five-year-old grandmother dancing to a Perry Como ditty with her recently widowed daughter, who happened to be my mother, hushed for a while the growing pangs of anger in my heart. I decided then and there I would cut God a little slack. I could tell he was trying hard to comfort me, and that meant a lot.

I replayed that dance in my head that early morning. I sat on the picnic table on the front lawn, waiting for the sun to rise. Everyone else slept, or so I thought.

As the sun rose over the ploughed fields of Butte Valley, I remembered one Easter when I was in high school. Fr. Gene Montoya, a Holy Cross priest from the University of Portland, came to our home with my brother Mike, then a freshman at the university, for the holiday. The whole family celebrated Mass that Holy Saturday night in our living room. Most memorable from that celebration was our communal butchering of Cat Steven's rendition of "Morning Has Broken," sung in more keys than there were singers.

"Mine is the sunlight, mine is the morning, born of the one light, Eden saw play," I sang softly on the farmhouse lawn. My voice cracked and quivered, but I forged ahead, thankful for the solitude. Like my brother's golf swing, my singing was a woeful and embarrassing display, but it was heartfelt.

God wants to be seen and heard

and touched and smelled and tasted,

for to be known by the senses

is to be loved.

I don't know what made me turn toward my mother's bedroom window, which looked out onto the lawn, but I did. She was standing there in her long flannel nightgown, wearing her black-rimmed glasses, so she knew it was me. She looked vulnerable and sad and so utterly human. She was singing along with me. But she was not alone. And neither was I. God was there with us.

This became a defining moment of revelation for me. I now know and believe with every fiber of my being that when sunlight warms the reddened cheek and mother and son steal a secret moment together at dawn, God is there. When brothers weep and laugh together on a golf course cut into fields of harvested October hay, and when sisters sing and dance with insouciance borne of a ferocious love that cannot be defeated, God is there. God is there in the smell of the musk caught in wool fabric and in the sound of a scratchy Perry Como LP. When joy beckons us to imbibe, God is there.

This is why God came from heaven to be with us in the first place: to join us in the drama of our lives...in the laughter and the tears, in the sunrises and the sunsets, in triumph and defeat. God wants to be seen and heard and touched and smelled and tasted, for to be known by the senses is to be loved. And more than anything else, God wants to be loved.

This is the enduring gift of the Incarnation, God becoming one-with-us. God is not far off, nor is God indifferent to our trials and tribulations. The truth of the Incarnation reminds us that God is close by, approachable and tangible. A friend once observed that the great tragedy of our time is that for too many people God has become painfully distant. "Here we are," he once told me, "walking in a downpour of Incarnation, and nobody's getting wet!"

The following stories speak of this enduring truth: we are all getting wet all the time, every single one of us. "God is in the bits and pieces of Everyday," Patrick Kavanagh once wrote, "A kiss here and a laugh again, and sometimes tears, a pearl necklace round the neck of poverty."

These are stories that speak of sacrament, the ancient belief that says in so many words that God can be tasted and touched and seen and heard and smelled. The Church teaches that Christ instituted seven sacraments so we could train our senses to see God coming down the road and hear his voice; feel his embrace; smell his musky, perfumed body; feast upon his countenance. These become the transforming moments of our lives worth retelling: stories of being washed clean and nourished, of being forgiven and enflamed, of being wedded in love and anointed for service, of being held and healed and made whole. These stories remind us that our story is God's story too. As someone once told me, the one thing we have in common with God is our humanity.

One evening many years ago, I was humbled by a sunset that recast my whole world in a soft, inviting, and healing light. I was for a short while unafraid of death, no longer intimidated by darkness, because like King David I had felt God's presence in a valley of tears. And the next morning, as I sung of a new dawn secretly with my mother, I knew that there was no turning back. Wherever I went, on whatever road I trod, God would be there, demanding nothing, simply enjoying—or at times enduring—the journey with me.

Patrick Hannon, CSC

ONE

Baptism: Living Water

In their distress, they will beg my favor:
"Come, let us return to the LORD;
for it is he who has torn,
and he will heal us;
he has struck down,
and he will bind us up.
After two days he will revive us;
on the third day he will raise us up,
that we may live before him.
Let us know,
let us press on to know,
the LORD;
his appearing is as sure as the dawn;
he will come to us like the showers,
like the spring rains that water the earth…."
For I desire steadfast love
And not sacrifice,
the knowledge of God
rather than burnt offerings.

Hosea 6:1-3, 6

I.

Coppertone, Chlorine,
and the Endless Summer

S tanding in line was the hardest part. Mom would drop us off at eight
in the morning that first day of summer vacation at the front entrance of the city pool, reminding us that she would be back to pick
us up at five. It was only years later that it struck me that Mom seemed to
speed away faster than the other moms, with the energy and enthusiasm
of a prisoner who had found a breach in the wall. Dropping nine kids off
for the day must have brought my mother a sense of deep and abiding
freedom few of us would ever understand.

So there we were, in a long line weaving its way around a gate whose
entrance wouldn't be unlocked for a half hour. From where the Hannon
kids stood we could see the high diving board dangling over the big pool.
We drooled over the sight of the blue, still water that filled the pool to
its brim. Coppertone lotion glistened on marble-white skin, transistor
radios blasted rock 'n roll, and the feeling of anticipation in the air was
thick. I was one of a hundred kids in line that first morning of summer;
and I'd bet every one of us wanted to forget everything, to leave the book
reports, the science projects, the vocabulary lists, the grammar drills,
and the schoolyard fights—all of it—behind. It was as if there was an
unwritten rule that morning: you may only talk about what you are going
to do, not what you have done. Talk that morning was of campouts in the
hills and trips to Disneyland, of baseball games and pranks planned on
unsuspecting neighbors. It was the horizon of fresh, blue, still water that
drew our attention, and nothing else.

The gate was unlocked promptly at eight-thirty; had the teenager
who opened the gate not gotten out of the way, he would have been
trampled underneath the asphalt-heated pitter-patter of two hundred
feet. Anyone who says we are not, at the core of our being, a people de-
pendent upon ritual has never been to a city pool on the first day of sum-

mer. We all staked out our territory first, placing towels and sandals and sodas on the grassy area next to the pool. We stripped to our swim suits and trunks and then made our way deliberately to the pool's edge, where a big toe was submerged to test the water. A smile would quickly crease our faces as one by one or in groups we jumped, dove, or cannonballed into the pool. For my part, I remember jumping into the deep end, feeling as my body pierced the surface of the water that every single thing in my eleven-year-old life was being washed away, that the Pat Hannon who jumped in and the Pat Hannon who climbed out dripping in the waters of a new summer were two different people.

My Batman and Robin lunch pail had begun gathering dust in the closet; memories of fights and feuds from school melted away; the smells of textbooks and playground asphalt were overpowered by the fragrances of summer. And though I never would have put it in these words then, it was as if my soul had been washed clean by the heavily chlorinated pool water. It was a new day and a new dawn. I knew it. We all knew it. The only thing that really mattered was the present day. It had been blessed by the water of summer.

Our horizon is the still, blue waters of renewed hope and promise. Everything else we leave at the water's edge.

Whenever I enter a Catholic church now, I remember those summer days of my youth as I reach for the holy water to bless myself. It is a holy gesture, a movement of the heart that seeks to bring all of us to a place of peace once again, for the waters of our baptism have never stopped flowing. God's favor still rests on us; we are God's beloved sons and daughters.

The past is prologue. We train our eyes on what is ahead and not on what is left behind. Our horizon is the still, blue waters of renewed hope and promise. Everything else we leave at the water's edge.

II.
Getting Wet

I t was a Sunday morning, maybe five, five-thirty. Mr. Rodriguez, the man in charge of us forty paper boys, hoisted the bright yellow Oakland *Tribune* burlap sack stuffed with rolled and rubber-banded newspapers onto the back rack of my bike just outside "The Shack," the place we assembled every day to get our newspapers. His tanned Portuguese skin tightened at the biceps as he lifted the sack, and I secretly prayed that someday I might be that muscular. I was ten years old, scrawny and thin, a bully's perfect target. This was the first Sunday that I was to be entrusted with my paper route all on my own. Past Sundays, Dad would rise early and take my brothers and me in the station wagon to deliver our papers and then treat us at Winchell's Donuts after the early morning Mass. But on that particular Sunday, I was there poised to ride into the darkness all by myself.

After Mr. Rodriguez secured my sack of papers to the back rack, he stepped back and I grabbed hold of the handlebars. Immediately, the bike reared back on its haunches and the front tire was now three feet in the air. Mr. Rodriguez took hold of the handlebars and wrestled the bike down so that the front wheel gently touched the asphalt. I climbed aboard hoping my meager frame would be a sufficient counterweight to my thick Sunday papers. By this time a dozen of the older, more seasoned paperboys were gathered around, enjoying the spectacle.

Mr. Rodriguez gave me a push, and I began pedaling very slowly. The bike crept along, first a little to the left, then a little to the right. I was exerting every ounce of my energy trying to keep the bike steady and moving. To the sound of whistles and guffaws, I wheeled away into the early morning darkness. At that exact moment, almost on cue, it began to rain. It was a downpour that within minutes had me soaking wet.

I arrived at my first customer's house on Chester Street. An older couple, they liked their newspaper tucked behind the front door screen. I dismounted my bike and immediately it tilted back and anchored itself to the pavement. What was a ten-year-old to do?

"Ah, shoot," I said. But I didn't say shoot. I said what my mother sometimes said when the casserole burned or when one of her children dragged yet another stray cat or dog into the house or when Dad came home from a fishing trip with a dozen trout to be gutted. I stood there facing the house like a drowned rat—a scrawny, skinny, little wet rat. "Shoot."

Ten minutes of thinking got me nowhere. I finally decided upon a bold move. I walked up to the front door of the house and rang the doorbell. I rang it again. I opened the screen door and knocked. Finally, I began pounding the door, until I saw a light turn on in the distant corner of the house.

An old lady in floppy slippers emerged from the shadows with her hair in curlers. She opened the door and inspected me. At that point, I safely concluded that words weren't really necessary. The woman could see me. She could see my bike. I turned and faced my bike so that together she and I could hear what the bike was saying: "Oh, my God!" My bike was laughing hysterically. "Can you believe it!" the bike said. "He is such an idiot! He's completely brainless!"

I turned back around and faced the woman, my face devoid of any emotion. She turned around and motioned me to the kitchen. I placed her Sunday paper on the table near the door and followed. She pointed to the phone on the wall as she shuffled to another room just off the kitchen. I dialed the number to my home.

"Hello, Mom?" I said. "Yeah, this is Pat. Pat, your fifth son? I'm at this house on Chester Street. Yeah. I can't seem to get back on my bike. I said, *I can't seem to get back on my bike.* Can you come and pick me up?"

At this point in the conversation, it must have finally dawned on my mother that she would have to get dressed and drive four miles to pick up her fifth son, just as she had retrieved her older children multiple times and would do the same for the younger ones when their time came.

Meanwhile, the old lady, whose sleep and house I had disturbed, came back with a big towel. "Turn the lights off and make sure the front door is locked when you leave," she said, as she walked away lethargically.

Thank God she didn't hear what my mother had to say on the other end of the phone.

"Shoot," she said. But she didn't say shoot. She told me she would be there in ten minutes. I turned the lights off in the kitchen and made sure the front door was locked as I gingerly stepped outside. I took the towel with me. It was hanging over my head. Years later my mother, recalling that day, told me that when she first saw me sitting there on the front stoop of the house with the towel draped over my head and my arms hanging over my knees, I looked like a washed-up old boxer. But at that moment when she pulled up to the curb, my heart leapt for joy: Mom had actually shown up.

We took my bike and put it in the back of the station wagon, and together we delivered the papers on my route. Later, we sat across from each other in a booth at Winchell's. I read the sports page and shoved maple bars into my mouth while my mother gulped coffee and smoked her cigarettes. She stared at me between puffs, and I became more than a little self-conscious.

And for a moment

that seemed to last forever,

I was the richest man in the world.

Was she about to use this private moment to inform me of my familial status (which my older brothers had already deliciously disclosed a few years before) that I was adopted? I looked up and flashed a smile that would make any woman swoon, but it had no immediate effect on Mom.

She grabbed her huge purse and began digging for something. I peered over the table to see what was going on. "Here it is," she said, and she handed me a shiny Eisenhower silver dollar coin. "I've been saving this for you," she told me. "I think now's as good time as any. Don't tell your brothers." And for a moment that seemed to last forever, I was the richest man in the world.

It was all worth it: the sweat, the toil, the humiliation, and that early morning baptism by which I had been somehow inexplicably, mysteriously reborn. I sat across from my mother, who had already moved on to another thought, another preoccupation, and I marveled at what the morning had wrought. I had been washed clean by a storm that had, in the end, washed me up on a new shore, leaving me wealthy beyond my imagination. I didn't care anymore what my bike thought of me. My bike had got it all wrong. I was not an idiot at all. I was my mother's son. And apparently my mother would go anywhere, do anything, to save me.

This I came to believe one Sunday morning when I was ten. I've never stopped believing it about my mother, or about God for that matter.

III.
Conquering Blood

Coming out of a movie theatre in San Francisco one evening, I turned my cell phone on and noticed my brother Brian had left four messages. They all were variations of the same theme: call me right away. My pulse quickened and my breath grew short as I fumbled with the phone. I knew whatever he had to tell me was not going to be good.

It wasn't. Our sister Mary's little five-year-old boy Michael was sick. She had taken him to the emergency room earlier that day because he had been running a fever and it wasn't going down. They ran tests and quickly diagnosed a leukemia of a rare and oftentimes lethal type when contracted at a young age.

I called Mary right away. Her voice was soft and reassuring and very matter-of-fact. She talked to me with a quiet ferocity that encouraged me. Like Meade before Gettysburg or Eisenhower before Normandy, my sister was calm, resolute, and angry. I might have almost felt sorry for the chronic myelogenous leukemia that had invaded little Michael's body if it weren't such a bastard of a disease. As it was, a little boy was sick, and his mother and father and their entire clan was immediately mobilized for battle.

Mary called me a few days later with a confession. Michael had never been baptized, and she sought to rectify the situation. She kept apologizing, seeing it as evidence of moral failure on her part. Good Catholic mothers baptize their babies; how could she have been so complacent, she was asking in so many words. But I didn't care. Mary had been working twelve hours a day at a grocery store in town; taking care of a chronically sick husband; feeding, clothing, and loving five children. I knew she had done quite well under the circumstances, and the postponed baptism would now take on extra significance.

Michael was baptized on a Saturday afternoon in October. The whole Hannon tribe—over thirty strong—gathered at the Downtown Chapel in

Portland. Michael's parents and brothers and sister and all of his aunts and uncles and a smattering of cousins surrounded him. I had spent the earlier part of the day with Michael, explaining what baptism signified for us Christians, but he was already way ahead of me, schooled as he was now in the vicissitudes of life and blessed with an untampered-with religious imagination.

"I am going to live forever," he said, "because I'm going to be washed clean by the blood of the Lamb." Where had he picked this lingo up I did not know. Not from me. I thought it was just a tad too esoteric for a boy of five. But he said it. And apparently he believed it too. A boy with weak, infected blood coursing through his veins was hitching his wagon to Jesus' star because somewhere he had heard that Jesus had good blood, healing blood, conquering blood, and that was good enough for Michael.

Maybe it began to dawn on him that for Christians tears are salty, holy prayers that burn the skin and cleanse the soul.

He was dressed in black trousers, a white shirt, and a clip-on tie. He approached the baptismal font, a boy wise beyond his years. He leaned his head over the font calmly, confidently, with a dancer's grace. He closed his eyes as I began. "Michael Patrick," I said as I poured water over his head, "I baptize you in the name of the Father, and of the Son, and of the Holy Spirit." As I said this, tears came to my eyes. Looking around I could see others crying as well. Michael was literally baptized with our tears.

Later that evening we all assembled at Old Town Pizza for dinner. Michael walked from table to table and soaked in the hugs and smiles, mystified still, I suppose, by the tears we had shed earlier that day at the church. Maybe it began to dawn on him that for Christians tears are salty, holy prayers that burn the skin and cleanse the soul. They water the desert and make fragile things grow.

These things Michael would come to know later. That night he ate pizza like it was manna from heaven and slugged down one root beer after another, as you would expect a little boy to do who is throwing himself into each meal as if it were his last.

Today, Michael is small in stature in his eleventh year because of the medication he takes. But he walks with giants, those holy men and women of whom John of Patmos once spoke, for Michael too has survived his time of great distress. His blood is strong now. He knows it. The chronic myelogenous leukemia knows it. He's going to live forever. He is a beautiful and fragile little boy, made strong by the blood of the Lamb.

TWO

Reconciliation: Healing the Breach

On this mountain,
The LORD of hosts will make for all peoples
a feast of rich food, a feast of well-aged wines,
of rich food filled with marrow,
of well-aged wines strained clear.
And he will destroy on this mountain
the shroud that is cast over all peoples,
the sheet that is spread over all nations;
he will swallow up death forever.
Then the Lord God will wipe away
the tears from all faces,
and the disgrace of his people
he will take away from all the earth,
for the LORD has spoken.

Isaiah 25:6-8

I.
The Long Yearning's End

It was November 12, 1978. The evening before, the eleventh, I had gone out to dinner with my girlfriend Kathy at the Spaghetti Factory in the Old Town neighborhood of Portland to celebrate my birthday. Kathy and I had begun dating during our junior year in high school. We had broken up for a brief time that year but managed to get back together for the junior prom. Then we broke up again soon after that.

By late spring of our senior year, however, we were back together again. I distinctly remember that romantic rapprochement at Jack London Square in Oakland. I had asked her out to dinner because I am a Hannon boy, and Hannon boys feel it is their particular vocation in life to make sure everyone is happy. We don't want anyone on the planet to feel bad for very long. I couldn't help but notice that Kathy was down in the dumps, so—as a friend—I suggested a meal at our favorite restaurant.

This was a huge mistake. As we strolled along the waterfront, the moon's reflection on the bay seducing us both into thinking that maybe, just maybe, our paths might converge once again, I realized that as much as I cared for Kathy I didn't love her. But I didn't have the guts to tell her. Not then. Not there.

The rest of the evening was a blur. We were standing together enjoying the view of the San Francisco skyline across the bay. All of a sudden Kathy was hugging me tightly and telling me how happy she was that we were back together. I don't know what I said to imply this, but it didn't really matter. Kathy was happy, so I was happy. "I'm happy too," I said. And I meant it. Then we kissed.

❋ ❋ ❋ ❋ ❋ ❋ ❋

It still came as somewhat of a shock to me a few weeks later when Kathy informed me that she had been accepted at the University of Portland. "Isn't this great!" she said as she snuggled up against me. "We're going to be at the same school!" It wasn't great, at least for me. Going to the University of Portland in the fall was my fail-safe plan. Kathy was supposed to stay home and go to Cal State in Hayward. We were supposed to be six hundred miles apart. Then we would of course quite naturally drift apart, and our relationship would go quietly into that good night. I had it all scripted.

"Yeah. Great." I said, hoping she would hear in the tenor of my voice the slightest hint of disappointment. She didn't.

The next thing I knew we were on a Greyhound bus, sitting together like an old married couple on our way to Portland, Oregon. Somewhere in the Siskiyou Mountains that old Simon and Garfunkel song came to mind as I stared out the window, Kathy fast asleep in the seat next to me. "Kathy, I'm lost, I said, though I knew she was sleeping. I'm empty and aching and I don't know why...." It felt like an out-of-body experience. I was watching myself on a half-lit stage, enshadowed and shrouded by a creeping darkness that was slowly gobbling me up.

We arrived at the University of Portland a few days before anyone else, and the rectors in our residence halls let us move in anyway. Later that first day, Kathy and I walked to the Fred Meyer store to buy our school supplies. It was a hot, balmy day. We passed front lawns scorched by the unforgiving sun and patches of tall weeds that hid abandoned tires and rusting shopping carts. Just before the turn to the Fred Meyer parking lot, we walked across an old steel bridge that spanned a series of railroad tracks below. As we neared the midpoint of the bridge, it began to shake. My California instincts kicked in, and I raced back to sturdy earth, convinced we were experiencing an earthquake.

Kathy stood where she was as I yelled for her to get off the bridge. She started laughing. She laughed so hard I thought she was going to bust a vein. There had been no earthquake. Large trucks crossing the bridge had caused the slight vibration on the bridge. Kathy waited for me to join her. She playfully needled me the rest of the way to the store, and most of the way back. Our relationship went downhill from then on.

We broke up for good the day after my birthday. The evening before, as I sat across from her at the Spaghetti Factory, I knew it was time. Kathy deserved someone who really loved her, who salivated at the thought that they might some day share a home, someone who daydreamed constantly of her soft kisses. The next morning, I called her on the phone and told her it was not going to work out, that we needed to say our goodbyes. Yes, I actually used those words. I wasn't very good at this. There was silence on the other end. I thought I heard a slight gasp and then sniffles. Then more silence.

"Kathy, are you there?" I said.

"Goodbye, Pat," she said. Then she hung up.

We didn't talk for weeks. Our paths occasionally crossed on campus, but even then we barely acknowledged each other. Every so often I would see her sitting in the dining hall with her friends. Kathy appeared to have moved on, but I was stuck in reverse, careening and plowing into remnants of my past, unable to avoid the evidence of my own cowardice, my fears, and my deep-seated insecurities that too often had me living what felt like a false, inauthentic life. I was completely alone and breathlessly lost.

One Saturday night later that fall, the guys next door in the dorm were having a big party. There must have been thirty students in their room, laughing and singing and drinking. Kathy was there. I could hear her, and—God is my witness—I could smell her perfume through the walls. It mocked me as I lay on my bed in the dark. On the radio, Barry Manilow was singing that schmaltzy tune "Weekend in New England," and when he reached that predictable Manilowesque crescendo, my fate was sealed. "When will our eyes meet, when can I touch you, when will this strong yearning end? And when will I see you again?" With that I burst into tears.

I was utterly alone in the world. I was nineteen years old, drifting on a very dark sea without anchor or compass or the North Star to guide me. Then it hit me. It wasn't Kathy I was pining for. She was a wonderful woman, but not my woman. Kathy would be fine. This was all about me. For maybe the first time in my short life, I was facing the terrible, awesome truth that no one person would ever save me from myself. It was not Kathy for whom my heart was beating furiously that night. My heart was yearning for God.

I saw Kathy one more time that semester before Christmas break. It was a Friday night. I was sitting by myself in the Commons, the university's dining hall. As I sat there contemplating my macaroni and cheese, a group of guys from my dorm approached my table surreptitiously and grabbed me from behind. They raised me high over their heads and began to chant my name, "Han-NON, Han-NON, Han-NON!" My God, I thought, they know who I am!

I wriggled and fought with all my might, but I was no match for their strong arms or their determination to wake up a sleepy night on the Bluff. Everyone in the Commons began to cheer and join the ever-increasing line that was making its way down the stairs to the huge water fountain that graced the terrace below.

In the echoing laughter and the cheering that night, I heard the voice of God telling me to get up and get on with the business of living.

It was a terrifying and exhilarating journey that night. As they tossed me into the ice-cold water of that fountain, I felt something deep inside loosen its grip on me, as if in defeat. As I fell into that water, I looked up and saw Kathy standing there, laughing so hard I thought she was going to bust a vein. Our eyes met, and we both smiled. I knew then that everything was going to be all right between her and me. All was forgiven. And in the echoing laughter and the cheering that night, I heard the voice of God telling me to get up and get on with the business of living.

II.
Hustled by a Holy Man

He was one heckuva billiards player. I'll give him that. He went by
the name of Felix. When I first met him back in 1984, I was a
naïve, trusting young man from California who was aspiring to
priesthood, who believed that deep down most every one was good and
noble and decent. That is not to say I had never witnessed the frailty of
the human condition. Being the scrawny runt of the Hannon family litter,
I experienced—on a weekly basis, it seemed—the cold and unflinching
calculus that rewarded strength and pitied weakness. When I wasn't being beaten into next week by one of my four older brothers, I was duking
it out with one of the bullies at school. Had I been born into a less civi-
lized time, certainly the tribe would have left me far behind to become
food for the vultures. As it was, however, I somehow managed to enter
adulthood with my optimism and my sense of fair play intact. I arrived
in Portland, Oregon, to begin my preparation for priesthood convinced
that all those years of fraternal fistfights and playground battles would
serve to make me the champion of the underdog, the strong voice for the
timid and the weak.

I met Felix at the old Estate Hotel, a fleabag flophouse that rented out
a few rooms to Sister Maria Francis, a Franciscan nun who ministered
to homeless men, women, and children in Portland. My seminary classmates and I were spending our summer in Portland working at various
social service agencies. My ministry was to give haircuts three days a
week at the Estate Hotel and the rest of the week to visit shut-ins. Felix was my first victim, er, I mean customer. Playing the professional I
wanted to be, I extended my hand to him when he first entered the room
that Monday morning for a haircut. As I took hold of his bony hand, I
asked him how he was.

Felix looked me over, took the measure of the boy in front of him,
and smiled back at the poor sucker he instinctively knew I was. A laughing and coughing fit ensued, one I was to become very familiar with over

the next six weeks. Felix was around sixty-five years old, but he looked to be eighty; he had grown up in Brooklyn and had celebrated his twenty-sixth birthday on the beach at Normandy. Somewhere on the road between Brooklyn and Normandy, Felix lost a wife, a home, a job, and his left eye. Along the way, he fell in love with the bottle, tobacco, and the smooth green felt of a billiards table. After I brushed the loose hairs off his shoulders and sprinkled his neck with talcum powder, Felix jumped out of the barber's chair, inspected my work, and finding it satisfactory, gave me a twenty five-cent tip. As he put on his old Brooklyn Dodgers jacket (his prized possession I was to find out) and made his way to the door, Felix let it be known that if I were ever free he'd be happy to shoot some pool with me.

Somewhere on the road between Brooklyn and Normandy, Felix lost a wife, a home, a job, and his left eye.

My heart leapt with joy at the invitation. I had been practically born with a pool cue in my hand, and Felix seemed like a man with a story to tell. Clearly this was God's handiwork and not my own. A week later, I was hanging out at a gin joint with my new friend Felix. We shot pool until three in the morning, pausing only those times when Felix's fake eye rolled across the pool table surface, having conveniently popped out of its socket just when I was about to sink the eight ball. Felix had been pulling stunts like that all night, trying to keep me off balance. He'd wink at me, or with a toothless grin hum some ditty from the forties, or start into one of his laughing and coughing fits. The thing was, by two in the morning, I had won every single game. And during that entire time, Felix was as sober as a Baptist preacher. I was about to call it a night when he begged me to play one last game. He suggested we make it interesting. The bet was this: I win, I get his Dodgers jacket; he wins, I give him twenty bucks.

You had to feel sorry for Felix. I had spent the better part of the evening and early morning showing off my obvious pool-playing prowess; the last thing I wanted to do was to embarrass him further. But he kept on asking and coughing and coughing and asking. I couldn't say no. But I decided that when I won I would tell him to keep the jacket. It was a cold night, and having been to his hotel room the day before, I knew it was one of the few possessions and the only jacket he owned. Something inside of me told me the jacket was the only evidence Felix had that there was a time when he lived for something other than the bottle. No, I would whip his behind again in pool—maybe even make him think it was close—and then tell him to keep the jacket. I knew then that I was going to make a great priest someday.

❖ ❖ ❖ ❖ ❖ ❖

Felix, as it turned out, had a very successful night of pool. He kept humming that same damned tune as he counted out the twenty bucks to make sure I hadn't shortchanged him. He kept on humming it as he bellied up to the bar to order what surely must have been the first of many whiskey shots that early morning, all paid for by the money he had hustled from me. You had to admire his patience and stamina. It may have been the longest time he had ever gone without a drink.

I kicked myself all the way back to my room that morning; how could I have been such a sucker? I tossed and turned for a few hours, unable to sleep, angry and ashamed and embarrassed. Around five in the morning I put on some old sweats and went for a walk around the Old Town neighborhood. The faintest hint of sunrise whispered of a new day, and yet around me all I saw was darkness. If a neighborhood could have a hangover, this one did, painted as it was in a hundred shades of despair. And I wasn't feeling very optimistic either. My first real venture into grime-and-grit ministry, and the only thing I had succeeded in doing was getting an old wino drunk and losing most of the money I had.

It was right about then, when I was feeling really sorry for myself, that the true story unfolded, the one that rarely gets told because so few of us are awake to see it. I suddenly saw Felix stumbling down the sidewalk, his bony hands buried deep in his pockets, his warm, wool Dodger's jacket buttoned all the way up to his chin. He was moving at a pretty fast clip, determined I suppose to outrun the cold, damp air. At one point, he stopped in front of an old storefront where a kid no older than sixteen or seventeen lay tightly curled and fast asleep. Felix stared down at the kid for a few seconds, and then he continued down the street. Then he stopped, made his way back to the storefront, and stared some more. He did this three or four more times—leaving and coming back—and it became clear to me that a very important conversation was going on in the heart of Felix that early morning. I leaned against a lamppost in the shadows and watched the drama unfold. On the last trip back to the kid, Felix stood there for what seemed like an hour but was probably only a minute. He unzipped his vintage Brooklyn Dodgers jacket, took it off, and placed it on the sleeping back of the boy huddled in that small corner. And then Felix left.

I know that when you distill this story down to the essential facts, what you have is that an old man too drunk to know any better was stupid enough to give away the one decent piece of clothing he had in his possession. Simply put, the weak got weaker. Those may be the facts; but it's not the truth.

The truth is that Felix was one heckuva pool player. He drank hard liquor and smoked unfiltered cigarettes and hustled naïve seminarians without as much as a hint of regret. And, in the end, he may have been one of the best teachers I ever had. For without having been trained as a preacher, early that morning Felix gave one of the best homilies I ever heard, one that spoke about how hope is born in the human heart. It comes to us silently and in secret and often when we least expect it. Handing over his coat to a cold stranger that early dawn, it was as if Felix had put flesh and bone and blood to the words Isaiah once spoke to a beaten and battered tribe: "Be strong, do not fear! Here is your God. He will come with vengeance, with terrible recompense. He will come and save you."

I was hustled once for twenty bucks by a pool shark masquerading as a friendly old wino. But by the crack of dawn I witnessed the hand of God—wrinkled and bony as it was—mend and heal. A young man woke up with a warm wool jacket; an old man went to sleep with a faint hint of hope dawning in his heart. And I went to church that morning, humbled by the fact that God's power often finds its greatest expression in weakness. I don't pretend to understand why this is so. But every now and then I think of Felix and how he became an instrument of my healing. He reminded me that God alone will satisfy the deepest hunger, quench the deepest thirst, and heal the deepest wound. He will do it secretly and silently, and when we least expect it.

III.
Lost at the Circus

I had heard enough stories in my short life to know that when you saw a kid running down the street to tell his buddies hanging out at the Tule Lanes Bowling Alley that the circus was coming to town, you better stand up and take notice. And that is what happened one summer day when my family and I were visiting Grandma Hannon on her farm in Tulelake, California. I had recently graduated from kindergarten and was still basking in the glory of mastering the alphabet and a portion of the multiplication tables and the names of all known barnyard animals. I had procured enough gold stars for good behavior that year to last me well into the fourth grade. So when I heard the news that the circus was coming to Tulelake, I thought that it was God's way of rewarding me for being such a good and obedient child and a loving son and brother.

I had never been to the circus before, but I always imagined it to be a mysterious world where flamethrowers and sword swallowers and trapeze artists dared us to match their cunning and courage. I imagined it to be a dangerous place where you brushed up against the breath of a crack-whipped lion, where you could be kissed by the wet trunk lips of a frisky elephant or have your hot dog stolen by a monkey if you didn't keep your head up. I imagined it to be a kind of daydream that a child could get lost in for a while, drawn as we all are by the taste of cotton candy, the smell of hay, and the sad charms of lonely clowns.

The traveling circus rolled into town that Wednesday evening; by Thursday you could see the big top towering over the Tulelake Horseradish Company, which stood adjacent to the county fairgrounds. On Friday evening I dragged my mother and my two younger sisters with me across the railroad tracks, through downtown, and past the high school to be one of the first to see the circus. Picture a little boy with a crew cut and big thick black glasses walking ten paces ahead of a woman trying to keep up, with two girls dangling from her arms and a cigarette dangling from her lips.

The line to get tickets was snaking around the huge white tent when we arrived. By the time we ducked our heads into the circus, it was already teeming with humanity. The first thing I saw was a boy not much older than I, a member of the circus family I surmised, walking a baby elephant toward some hay. The nonchalant, I've-done-this-a-million-times-before expression on his face fascinated me to no end and got me to imagining how I could shake off the shackles of my little life and make this boy my brother. Seeing my mother juggle my little sisters, a cigarette, and three small popcorns, I realized she could only take me so far in life. If I were to make it in this world at all, I would have to do most of the heavy lifting. Still, I hovered close to my mother, never straying far from her maternal shadow. It was then that it first dawned on me that though I was old enough to dream I had not yet acquired the necessary bravery to act on those dreams; and so I clung to my mother that Friday evening, even as my heart was walking baby elephants, balancing on the tight-rope, and sleeping under the stars.

I lost Mom as the clowns were riding their big-wheeled bikes like lunatics around the three rings of the circus. They were throwing candy into a mob of children, and I was determined to get my fair share. I surfaced from the feeding frenzy to find that I recognized absolutely no one. I looked left; I looked right. I walked ten paces to the north, then ten paces to the south. I pretended to not be lost, because I didn't want anyone to think I was stupid enough to get lost in the first place, but inside my heart was racing, and on the horizon of that beating little heart a storm of pure panic was gathering. Nothing—not books that had been read to me, nor movies, nor the television programs I had studied, nor late-night conversations with my brothers, nor even the field trip to the Castro Valley Fire Station that spring—had prepared me for the horror of discovering that when you get lost at a circus, you probably will never be found. It was a heavy existential truth that barged into my life, and for a while I was lost in a nightmare I thought would never end.

It was obvious that I would be joining the circus the next day; no other possibility presented itself to my untested six-year-old intellect that night. They would probably make me change my name: "Patrick" didn't seem very circus-worthy. "Marvin" or "Brutus" or "Clyde," maybe. I'd have to start at the bottom, cleaning out cages and hosing down elephants at first and then working my way up. Oh, sure, my mother and father, my brothers and sisters would miss me for a week, maybe a month, but eventually they would come to appreciate the extra potato in the stew and the newly freed-up square-footage I had once occupied and move on with their now empty lives. But I would never forget them, I remember thinking; and I conjured up their faces with my mind's eye so I would always remember what they looked like.

❖ ❖ ❖ ❖ ❖ ❖

It was when I pictured my mother in my mind that I started to cry; and it wasn't because I missed her that I wept. No, at that point I was crying because I was angry with her, for it was not I who lost her but she who lost me. Mom had broken the rules. I had been an obedient— well, a mostly obedient—son. I was clearly her favorite. I had kept my part of the bargain. She was supposed to have kept hers and not lose me. How could she have been so absent-minded and hard-hearted as to leave me at the mercy of flame throwers and sword swallowers and women with beards?

I just remember how being lost almost swallowed my heart whole.

I don't remember how Mom and my sisters found me that night, but obviously they did. I don't remember a happy reunion, or the tears of a mother bathed in relief, or the sweet, intoxicating fragrance of the pillow as I slept in my own bed later that night. I just remember how being lost almost swallowed my heart whole. Forty-three years later, I'm still turning the soil of that memory, trying to unearth a gemstone that will shine light on the mystery of those little deaths we all endure that leave us like children lost at a circus.

THREE

Eucharist: Transformation

"Very truly I tell you,
unless you eat the flesh of the Son of Man
and drink his blood,
you have no life in you.
Those who eat my flesh
and drink my blood
have eternal life,
and I will raise them up on the last day.
For my flesh is true food
and my blood is true drink.
Those who eat my flesh
and drink my blood
abide in me,
and I in them.
Just as the living Father sent me,
and I live because of the Father,
so whoever eats me will live because of me.
This is the bread that came down from heaven,
not like that which your ancestors ate,
and they died.
But the one who eats this bread
will live forever."
John 6:53-59

I.
Come for the Chicken, Stay for the Redemption

My family moved into the house on Knoll Way in the summer of 1971. We had long outgrown the Arcadian Drive house, with Mom, Dad, nine kids, a Chihuahua, and five cats residing in a four-bedroom house. The tipping point, I suppose, was the day Mom announced that her mom, Grandma Lighthouse, was going to move in with us. Our reaction must have confused our mother when she told us, because as delighted as we were at the thought of Grandma living with us—what with her hearty laugh, great stories, and the magical quality to her cooking—we could do the math. One of us was going to have to sleep in the garage to make room for her. A few short weeks later, Mom and Dad informed us we were moving to a bigger house, one with a swimming pool no less, on the other side of town. So it was that I came to live next door to a girl my age named Cathy Beevis, who a few months later, on a cool October evening, was to show me the face of God.

I first met Cathy and her brother a few days after moving in. My brothers and sisters and I were playing "Marco Polo" in our swimming pool when I noticed Cathy and her brother leaning over the fence that separated our two backyards. Mom was out on the balcony, and in her attempt to get us to mingle more with our new neighbors she had invited them over for a swim. This would happen dozens of times that first summer as word got out in the neighborhood that the goofy Hannon family would share their pool with anyone who would say "hello" to them. We had kids hanging from trees and fences like monkeys that summer.

✤ ✤ ✤ ✤ ✤ ✤

"I think Cathy likes you," my mom informed me one morning while I was sitting at the kitchen table eating my cornflakes. "I think she's a very nice girl, don't you?"

My heart sank at hearing those words. It was always the first salvo in Mom's campaigns to get one of my older brothers hitched. I don't know what had gotten into her that summer, but she was happily ensconced in matchmaker mode, letting my brothers and I know that she was keeping her eyes open for us.

As far as Mom was concerned, one of us had to become a priest, and the others were going to get married and give her lots of grandchildren. Apparently my mother had me pegged as one of the married men. Years later, my brother Michael, then a father of seven, told me that about that time Mom had hinted that *he* was to be the priest. Mike's wild, passionate romance with Heidi Densler during his seventeenth summer, however, disabused Mom of that notion.

Cathy did seem to spend a lot of time over at our house, but I thought it was because my older sisters had adopted her. Then I began to put two and two together. Who always seemed to be lying next to me on the poolside concrete as I was drying off after a swim? Cathy Beevis. Who always answered the door when I stopped by their house at the end of the month for collection time on my paper route? Cathy Beevis. Who was always at her bedroom window looking out at three-thirty in the afternoon when I was returning home from school? Yep. Cathy Beevis. This evidence troubled me. I was convinced that Cathy and my mother were in cahoots. Honest to God, if I had come home unexpectedly one day only to find the two of them sitting at the kitchen table sharing a pot of coffee, I would have moved to Canada and been done with it.

I was a twelve-year-old boy just trying to survive one day to the next. The last thing I needed was a meddling mother or the girl next door hanging all over me. So I kept my distance from both of them that summer and early fall, confident that whatever feelings Cathy might have for me of a romantic nature would die from benign neglect.

❖ ❖ ❖ ❖ ❖ ❖ ❖

One evening in October while I was watching television in the living room, the doorbell rang. I slowly got up from the floor to answer it, but my mother darted ahead of me and beat me to the door. It was Cathy Beevis.

"Pat," Mom said, "Cathy is here to see you." As Mom walked past me on her way back to the kitchen, she gave me a look that communicated clearly, "You'd better be nice to her."

Cathy had come over to invite me to her church picnic that Friday night. She belonged to a small Christian church in Hayward that liked to whoop it up just about every night. I'd pass that church on my bike with my brother on our way back home from toilet-papering someone's house or after enjoying a few games at the bowling alley, and we could hear them praising Jesus and singing and dancing. I thought they were all lunatics. We'd come home and mimick them at dinner: "Praise the Laaaawd and pass the potatoes! Thank you, Jesus!" In the beginning this would throw our mother off, for on the one hand we were invoking the name of our Lord and savior, but on the other hand Catholics never invoked the name of our Lord and savior outside of Mass.

Secretly I felt a twinge of sadness,

toward whom—them or me—

I had not yet discovered.

I remember riding by Cathy's church one early Sunday afternoon on my bike just as the people were coming out. I had gone to the seven-thirty morning Mass, so by the time the evangelicals were done praising Jesus I had put in a full day: work on the tree fort with my friend Steve, lunch at the International House of Pancakes, a trip to the flea market. I saw Cathy walking with her mom and dad and older brother, all of them in their Sunday's best, clinging to their black-leather Bibles, smiles of contentment on their faces. Secretly I felt a twinge of sadness, toward whom—them or me—I had not yet discovered.

❖ ❖ ❖ ❖ ❖ ❖

"Um," I said, as I frantically searched that night for a plausible reason to regretfully decline Cathy's invitation. I glanced toward the kitchen and my mother was mashing the potatoes, showing off her biceps and staring at me through those black-rimmed glasses of hers.

"Sure," I said, and Cathy smiled that crooked-teeth smile of hers and skipped out of our home and all the way back to hers. It took all of thirty seconds for the news to reach the far end of the house. For the rest of the week my brothers and sisters tormented me: "Cathy and Pa-at sitting in a tree...."

I fought with my mother that week more than I had my entire life. I moaned and groaned and whined and pleaded, all to no avail. Friday morning as I got out of the station wagon at school, I played my last card. "I don't even like her," I said. "She's so, so, ugly." My mother looked at me as if suddenly she no longer knew who I was. She drove off without saying a word.

At five o'clock that Friday night I walked across our front lawn to Cathy's house where she greeted me with a delightfully red face that stood in stark contrast to my sullen own. My brothers and sisters said goodbye to me with their sarcastic hands folded in prayer as the Beevis family and I drove off to an evening church picnic. Praise Jesus.

❄ ❄ ❄ ❄ ❄ ❄

I have to admit the fried chicken was good. Really good. We sat at a table, all crunched together and surrounded by thirty or forty other families. At first I used my fork and knife, because everyone else was using theirs. It was my opinion that fried chicken was one reason God blessed us with hands, but apparently this was not the case. Once again it became plainly obvious to me that we Hannons were Philistines, uncouth and uncivilized. Cathy, sensing my frustration and near-humiliation, however, grabbed a chicken leg with her delicate hands (I had never noticed how porcelain-white and dainty they were) and took a boisterous bite out of it. Her mother shot a disapproving glance her way, but Cathy was not intimidated. I then grabbed some chicken and did my best to stuff as much of it into my mouth as was humanly possible.

This amused Cathy to no end, and she let out a laugh that I think surprised even her and sent chunks of semi-chewed chicken flying from her mouth across the table. This, in turn, sent me into a laughing fit I could not stop, even when snot started snorting from my nose. This did not amuse Cathy's mother or her father one bit, or her older brother for that matter.

Later that evening, after all the fried chicken and mashed potatoes and coleslaw had been eaten, everyone went upstairs to the main body of the church to sing and praise Jesus. For some reason, I sang like someone who had been born again, and when the preacher announced an altar call I went down and let the preacher pray over me. Because you see, it suddenly struck me like a two-by-four across the head that the tinge of sadness I had felt when I had seen everyone come out of Cathy's church that early Sunday afternoon a few weeks earlier had been for me.

I was feeling sad for myself because, even at age twelve, I realized I was in danger of going blind. Beauty abounds in this world because God created all of it, and all of us, with beauty in mind. And I knew I was slowly losing sight of that truth, surrendering myself to the conventional wisdom that beauty really is only skin-deep. That night at Cathy's church with her family and their well-mannered friends and their delicious chicken, my eyes were open to human beauty that delights and pleases and triumphs precisely because it reveals the ultimate truth that lives just beneath the surface of things. It is our awareness of this beauty that makes us most human and only a little less than the angels. We look at one another, and every so often we see what I saw that night when Cathy spewed fried chicken across the table: I saw the face of God.

We look at one another,

and every so often we see

what I saw that night

when Cathy spewed fried chicken

across the table:

I saw the face of God.

My job, at age forty-nine, is to remember that face.

II.
A Motley Crew

It is a cool October morning, mellow and dreamy-like, and here I am celebrating mass at Cedar Woods, a care facility on the west side of Colorado Springs. Therese, one of our pastoral ministers to the homebound, is standing right next to me. She's a spry sprig of a lady, prone to hugging anyone that moves, and when she does she grabs hold of them in a way that says in no uncertain terms: *I love you, but don't mess with me; I'm a mother of nine.* Therese just turned eighty years old, and she's tough in a very sweet way.

Collected around one of the tables—our makeshift altar—are six other residents, a menagerie of delicate creatures in their wheelchairs locked in place. There's Irish Mary, a Dublin girl, who serenades me with "Danny Boy" after every Mass. There's Harry, a blind, cantankerous old coot with plastic rosary beads draped around his neck. "Who's there?" he barks every five minutes or so. There's Evelyn, big-boned and bigger-bosomed. She carries herself with a matriarchal air. I see her in her natural state, resting in her rocker on a wide front porch on a late Sunday afternoon in bygone days, peeling potatoes for supper and surveying the quiet neighborhood and finding it all acceptable.

There's Jane with her hands hidden under a shawl on her lap because they are gnarled now and, apparently in her eyes, unbecoming; and there's Sophia, whose eyes are always closed and you think she is fast asleep. Sophia opens her eyes only twice at Mass: first when she receives communion and second when I say goodbye at the end. She grabs my hand and says, "Come back again, Father. Please don't forget us." Her eyes are ocean blue, irises blessed and burdened by the soft imprint of every wound and tickle this world has ever given her.

Olivia also has blessed us with her presence again. I'm pretty sure Olivia is Catholic, but she has Pentecostal tendencies. When the Holy Spirit moves her, she speaks with a tongue free of any attempt at self-control. Today, while I am wishing everyone peace after the Our Father, she says, "Father Pat, if you don't stop smiling like that, people are going to think you are retarded."

✿ ✿ ✿ ✿ ✿ ✿

I am praying the Eucharistic Prayer of the Mass, and I swear to God Therese is murmuring the words too. She is standing right next to me, her arms extended outward, like mine. Well, at least one hand is. The other is extended also, but it is connected to one of Jane's hands that Therese has managed to liberate from its knitted pall. Jane has the look of confusion painted on her face, but then at some point she figures "what the heck" and takes her other bony hand and reaches across to Evelyn's hand and grabs it. And Evelyn purposefully takes her free hand and reaches across the great divide that separates her chair from Sophia's and grabs hold of Sophia's hand, who then, with eyes closed, reaches over to where she thinks Olivia is supposed to be and starts pawing her shoulder. Olivia squeals "Praise Jesus!" and grabs Sophia's hand and reaches over to Mary. Mary has been observing this wave of connecting hands drawing toward her and anticipates it with a near-toothless grin and her own right hand, and it looks like the hand of Michaelango's Adam as it stretches to meet the hand of God, as if her whole life depends upon touching Olivia. And finally, Mary reaches out her hand to Harry, who may very well have been asleep but is awakened by a warm hand on his. "Who's there?" he says.

We are in our own ways clinging to our humanity while claiming our share of God's divinity

✿ ✿ ✿ ✿ ✿ ✿

What a motley holy crew we are: incongruous, colorful, foolish. We are in our own ways clinging to our humanity while claiming our share of God's divinity—a gritty grace that makes dull things shine and dead things live.

After Mass I say my last goodbye and Mary, Olivia, and Sophia are wheeled away to their hair appointments. Evelyn sighs with satisfaction and Jane crawls back under her shawl as they are transported off to their rooms. And I can hear Harry still shouting "Who's there?" as he makes his way back to his secular-monk's cell with its singular bed. Therese and I come to an intersection in the hallway. She turns left and I turn right; she to visit a few more bed-bound Catholics and I to my car. I am smiling, I know. What others might conclude from my grin I dare not guess, but, if they cared to ask, this is what I would tell them: I can't seem to shake the memory of the sacred table prayer the eight of us just prayed, when we were all holding hands for dear life. I can't help thinking that this must have been what the Last Supper was like.

III.
The Measure of Love

Two weeks before Sister Delfina saw fit to promote her class to the fifth grade, a class that was her "forty-five reasons to pray and pray often," Mr. Silva, our janitor, died. He had come to America as a child from Portugal and settled with his immigrant tribe in the East Bay of California. His father, as Mr. Silva told a group of us once when he was throwing trash into the incinerator, was a direct descendent of the famous Portuguese explorer Bartholomew Dias, who, as we had learned in school that year, was the first European to sail around the southern end of Africa in 1488. Such rich, adventurous blood had been distilled down through the generations, until it coursed through the veins of the simple man dressed in denim overalls standing before us, tossing half-eaten apples, egg cartons, construction paper, and old magazines into a fiery furnace.

Mr. Silva lived with his wife in a little bungalow not far from the church. Saturday afternoons I would often pass by their house on my way to the bowling alley and see him tending to his garden or the old jalopy that leaked oil on the driveway. His short-cropped, grayish-white hair stood in stark contrast to his dark-leathered laborer's skin. His wife would often be sitting in a chair on the front porch shucking corn or knitting or saying her rosary. I thought they made a lovely couple. It troubled me, even as a nine-year-old, to think that Mrs. Silva was now alone.

We were all impressionable kids back then; so when Sister Delfina entered our classroom that morning to tell us of Mr. Silva's death, her face ashen and peculiar, so unlike her normal marine-drill-instructor self, we took notice. Being children, immortal and untouched by death, we were startled that someone we actually knew, like Mr. Silva, could die in the first place. Who would be mopping up Monica Fowler's spit-up the next time she decided to eat the world's largest banana? Who was going to perform simple maintenance repairs on our bikes during the school day? Who was going to inspect the pounded-out blackboard erasers after we had finished "cleaning" them?

Except for these tasks or occasional sightings at the incinerator, none of us could remember seeing Mr. Silva do his work. He locked the doors at dusk, long after we had departed, and unlocked them in the morning, while we were still reading the back of the Wheaties cereal box and munching on our breakfast toast at home. The bottom line was that he kept our learning environment clean, and now he was dead.

❖ ❖ ❖ ❖ ❖ ❖

Mr. Silva's was the first funeral most of us had ever attended. I remember the march over to the church from school; all 350 of us, eight grades, eight very straight lines, converging on poor Mr. Silva on the only school day he probably ever had off. My friend Lance and I decided the nuns were making us go so that at least there would be someone to see Mr. Silva off to God. Other than his immediate family, who else would go to the funeral of a janitor? I figured it would be an even trade: we pray for Mr. Silva's soul and he gets us out of our math quiz. It was with such cold calculation that I entered the church.

I figured it would be an even trade: we pray for Mr. Silva's soul and he gets us out of our math quiz.

Mrs. Medioti was pounding away at the organ with some dark and depressing dirge of a prelude, and the sweet smell of incense greeted us as we passed through the huge wooden doors of the church. Inside, we were confronted with the first evidence of Mr. Silva's greatness: except for the first nine or ten pews, into which the entire school population would be jammed for the duration, every possible seat was occupied. People stood all along the sides; some even braved climbing the narrow stairs up into the organ loft. Mr. Silva, it appeared, had done more than just clean toilets all his life. So there we sat, Sr. Delfina's forty-five reasons to pray, having made a fundamental error by thinking that to be successful you have to be important and famous and in the limelight, that you have to have a job that "counts" (or at least pays a lot).

Mr. Silva had come into this world quietly, as light as a feather floating to the earth, a babe in the arms of his mother, who must have seen him for what he truly was: a miracle. And he left quietly, in the arms of another woman, his wife, who must have wept in painful wonder at how one man could touch her soul so completely. Between his coming and his going, under us kids' very noses, Mr. Silva lived a heroic life.

❀ ❀ ❀ ❀ ❀ ❀

It was years later when I finally understood why there was such a huge throng to see Mr. Silva off to paradise. Like many unsung laypeople in our church, I'm sure he embodied all that was good and kind and generous in humanity. He was a holy man, possibly a descendent of a great Portuguese voyager, who was content to explore the landscape of the human heart, seeking adventure in the journey of simple human loving, all confined within the borders of one zip code. It is a humbling truth for priests like me to consider. Our congregations are full of people like Mr. Silva, who incite all of us to glory and greatness of the most enduring kind, the kind measured in love and nothing else.

FOUR

Confirmation: Lighting a Fire

When Jesus came to Nazareth,
where he had been brought up,
he went to the synagogue on the sabbath day,
as was his custom.
He stood up to read,
and the scroll of the prophet Isaiah was given to him.
He unrolled the scroll
and found the passage where it was written:
"The Spirit of the LORD is upon me,
because he has anointed me
to bring glad tidings to the poor.
He has sent me to proclaim release to the captives
and recovery of sight to the blind,
to let the oppressed go free,
to proclaim the year of the LORD's favor."
And he rolled up the scroll,
gave it back to the attendant
and sat down.
The eyes of all in the synagogue looked intently at him.
Then he began to say to them,
"Today this scripture has been fulfilled in your hearing."

Luke 4:16-21

I.
"That Ain't Right"

Mr. Rodriguez, the fellow in charge of us newspaper boys, told me one day that I could sell liquor to a nun. I took it as a compliment. I was only fourteen years old and had already developed a reputation among the newspaper carriers in my town for selling new subscriptions to our hometown paper, the Oakland *Tribune*. I had earned enough points from new subscriptions to win several trips to Disneyland and one to San Diego, a new bike, matching black-and-white portable television sets (I gave one to my grandmother, who had moved in with us), and more besides.

I had several things going for me. I was a puny kid with big ears, a face full of freckles, and a disarming smile. God and genetics engineered it thus to give me a fighting chance at survival in a family of nine and a grade school filled with short-tempered boys named Clancy and Quinn and Halloran. I could be a real charmer when circumstances required it.

I also could talk. Words came naturally to me, and I used them in a way that impressed older folks. Earlier that year, for my eighth grade graduation, Grandma had given me Webster's *New Collegiate Dictionary*. It became my sword, my shield, and my syllabic armor.

One Sunday afternoon, about the time Mr. Rodriguez suggested I might have a career in bootlegging, I approached my dad after our beloved Oakland Raiders had fallen to the Denver Broncos. He was slumped in his green leather chair in the living room with a look on his face his children knew all to well. Dad never took kindly to a Raider loss, so we usually kept our distance for a few hours, lest he unleash the wrath he intended for Stabler, Biletnikoff, or Casper on us.

This day, though, I walked right up to him, armed only with my fledgling vocabulary, put my hand on his shoulder, and said something like, "Dad, don't be so lugubrious. We'll beat 'em next time." Dad gave me a strange look. He stared at me and chuckled. He hoisted himself up from his chair with his signature grunt, rolled the newspaper up, and gently swatted me on the head.

❀ ❀ ❀ ❀ ❀ ❀ ❀

The secret to my success as a newspaper subscription salesman was to go to the poorest neighborhoods in Oakland and never take "no" for an answer. Weeknights, Mr. Rodriguez would drive us to East Oakland and drop us in front of a row of apartment buildings with assurances that he would return in an hour. My buddy Jason and I would begin at the top floor of the buildings and work our way down, steady-paced and efficient, like field hands bringing in the harvest.

The two of us helped each other hone our sales pitches so that they were virtually irresistible. We came armed with two-for-one deals, discounted magazine offers when attached to a three-month newspaper subscription, whatever we needed to sweeten the deal. We were pure poetry in action. I could tell within ten seconds if the person in front of me was going to take the bait. If I sensed even the slightest possibility of a sale, I would very slyly place my foot near the door so they couldn't close it; then I would turn on the charm until they were putty in my hands.

The abject poverty was unlike anything I had ever experienced in our cocoon-like suburban tract of homes.

Forget for a moment that few of the people in the "projects" could actually *afford* a subscription. Often the man or woman at the door would invite me in as they filled out the subscription form. I would notice empty cupboards, emaciated kids, broken-down furniture, curled-up linoleum, and the occasional rodent. The abject poverty was unlike anything I had ever experienced in our cocoon-like suburban tract of homes.

I remember once sitting in the living room of a woman who lived in one of those apartment buildings. She had her little girl in a playpen in the kitchen. As the woman was filling out a subscription form, my eyes met the little girl's. She was maybe two years old. Her kinky-black hair was brushed into two pigtails, and she wore a beautiful white dress that only accentuated her richly dark skin. As the little girl observed me, I began to make funny faces, and her eyes grew wide as if she were witnessing something exotic and magnificent. She let out a loud giggle that drew her mother's attention. When she caught me in the act of yet another funny face, she said, "You flirtin' with my little girl?" I grew red with embarrassment.

The mother just guffawed and went on scribbling on the pad in front of her. The little girl reached down in her playpen and grabbed her doll, leaned over the edge, and handed it to me. I took hold of the grimy little thing with drool stains all over it and held it for a few moments. It was the ugliest thing I had ever seen, but as I inspected the room in which I sat, I noticed nothing of comparable worth. It was as if most everything in this woman's life had been stripped away and reduced to its bare essentials: a little baby girl with captivating eyes and a grungy doll reduced to a soggy rag by so much love.

But all I could think about at the time was that this subscription would put me over the top. I had earned another trip to Disneyland.

❊ ❊ ❊ ❊ ❊ ❊

Later that year, about Christmastime, Jason and I took the bus on a Saturday back into East Oakland to do some more soliciting. We were both racking up the points that day and were delirious with excitement. Toward the end of the day, I caught up with Jason standing at a door talking with a young woman who was leaning against the doorframe, her arms folded in front of her while she listened intently to Jason's pitch. Jason was in his element. It was fun watching him reel in another one.

"Why don't you boys come on in," she said, "I need a cigarette." We sat down on the couch in the living room while the lady lit a cigarette and began fishing in her purse for something. She took out a wad of dollar bills and said, "Now how much do I owe you?"

Jason said, "Ma'am, you don't pay us; you'll pay your paper boy at the end of the month." I was impressed by Jason's honesty. As this was going on, I was looking around and taking note of the usual squalor. She had put up a Christmas tree in the corner by the window, but only a few ornaments hung from its branches. No lights, no tinsel. I suppose she thought that something was better than nothing, but I found it all a little depressing. A wave of sadness washed over me, and all I wanted to do was leave, catch the next bus, and head back to the suburbs. (It is true what T.S. Eliot once wrote: "Humankind cannot stand very much reality.") But a sale was a sale, so I stuck around.

A wave of sadness washed over me, and all I wanted to do was leave, catch the next bus, and head back to the suburbs.

The lady had a little boy, six or seven years of age. He emerged from a back room and made his way to the living room. He was all head and trunk, with tiny little fins for arms and no legs to speak of. He rolled and scooted his way to the base of the Christmas tree as if he had arranged to have something delivered there. His mother kept filling out the subscription form as the boy rustled under the tree and shook the two lone wrapped boxes for clues. Bored by the paucity of presents, he pivoted, deftly made his way to Jason and me, and began staring at our feet and legs.

"You know what I asked Santa for Christmas?" the boy asked us.

His mother, taking a drag from her cigarette, said as she exhaled, "Jason, you know what I told you about that." But little Jason was not going to be deterred.

"Legs!" he said. "Santa gonna bring me legs!"

That was it for me. I felt slightly sick to my stomach. I gave big Jason a look that said I wanted to leave, and in a few minutes we did. Neither of us said anything until we got to the bus stop. Words escaped me, and Jason was clearly very upset by what we had seen. It had left both of us desolate, almost gasping for air.

"That ain't right," Jason kept on saying on the bus all the way home. "That just ain't right."

❀ ❀ ❀ ❀ ❀ ❀ ❀

A couple of days before Christmas, on a Saturday, Jason called my house at five in the morning. He knew I would be up getting ready to go down to the Shack to pick up my papers for my route that morning.

"I need your help, Pat" he said. "Meet me at my house in ten minutes." He spoke in a voice I had never heard before, one that I could not ignore or refuse or even question.

He was waiting for me on the front stoop of his house and motioned me to come in. In the darkness of his living room, I could make out the family Christmas tree decked out with all the usual ornaments, plus popcorn strings and paper icicles and construction paper loops of red and green. There was a little nativity scene tucked near the base of the tree and, as I expected, the manger was empty, waiting for Jesus on Christmas day. Around the base were already lots of presents.

"Give me a hand," he said. "Grab the ones that have my name on them. There should be five."

"What's going on?" I whispered. But Jason wasn't answering. We carried the packages outside and to our bikes, balanced them on the baskets on our handle bars, and together careened down his street on our way to Mission Boulevard, which, when you get to the San Leandro border, becomes East 14th Street, which eventually takes you into East Oakland and to one particular apartment building and a woman who had a boy named Jason who thought Santa was going to bring him legs for Christmas.

❀ ❀ ❀ ❀ ❀ ❀ ❀

I didn't say a word the entire way, and that might be a record for me to this day. I spent the hour or so it took us to get to that apartment building thinking about my buddy on the bike next to me and wondering what had possessed him to do something so outrageously heroic. And then, of course, it finally hit me. Little Jason, his namesake, with his little arm flippers and no legs to speak of, rolling around on the dirty carpet with a big smile on his face as if it were the most natural thing in the world to do had said, "Legs! Santa gonna bring me legs!"

I don't think little Jason realized the role he was playing in this hidden drama unfolding in my friend Jason's mind and heart, but at that very moment, I am convinced, big Jason was forever, wonderfully, magnificently ruined. He would never—could never—be the same. He had unlocked the true meaning of Christmas.

We dropped off the five presents in front of little Jason's apartment door and rang the doorbell around a dozen times before high-tailing it out of there. Riding side-by-side on the still quiet city street, Jason looked over to me and said, "You tell anyone about this, and I will kill you." I never did, until now. I changed his name though. If I didn't, I know he would still kill me.

II.
The Banjo Man

I go to churches and ballparks for pretty much the same reason: because God is there. You'd think that this admission would cause my sainted Irish-Catholic mother to roll in her grave, but really she's the one to blame. It was my mother who carried me into Our Lady of Grace Church for the first time when I was a baby, and she was the one who took me to my first Oakland Athletics baseball game. I don't remember my first day of church, but I do remember my first trip to the ballpark on Heggenberger Road just off the Nimitz Freeway in Oakland, California. It was on a Wednesday night in July 1968. That evening of grace and baseball is stitched into my memory forever.

❀ ❀ ❀ ❀ ❀ ❀

My mother took me to see the new Oakland A's play Denny McLain's Tigers that warm night because I was apparently the only one of her brood who deserved to go. At least that's what I inferred as we drove together to pick up her younger brother, my Uncle Bernard, before we met up with my Uncle Jim and Aunt Rose at the ballpark. All the way to Bernard's, my mother was spitting fire. God only knows what my miscreant siblings had done, but I distinctly remember my mother looking over at me in the passenger seat, her sanity hanging from a thread, and saying with her weary eyes, "You, Patrick, you are my last hope."

My brothers and sisters might take issue with this remembrance, but they weren't there. As God is my witness, my mother—gripping the steering wheel with white knuckles, her diminutive frame leaning forward as if she were steeling herself for the final battle—bestowed on me a gift that I could only have concluded then (as I do now) was meant for the One Who Was Chosen. No longer could my brothers tease me into a fight by insisting I was adopted. Long ago I had concluded I was my father's favorite. Now, apparently, I was my mother's as well!

❀ ❀ ❀ ❀ ❀ ❀

And then there was this crazy bearded man with a banjo. I never knew his name. Never knew where he lived. Never knew a single thing about him except that he wore a scraggly red beard that cascaded down to his knees (or so it seemed); that he wore a cape with a huge, kelly green calligraphied "A's" stitched onto a golden satin background; and that he played the banjo like nobody's business. I saw him there at the ballpark hundreds of times since that night in 1968, but the first time I laid eyes on him I literally ran into him, or he into me. I had raced ahead after surrendering my ticket to the lady at the turnstile, so excited was I to breathe for the first time the fragrances only baseball parks can produce: the smells of hot dogs and cotton candy and spilled beer, of fresh sod and half-smoked cigars and wooden bleachers. I was so transfixed by those first whiffs of professional baseball, and my gaze was so affixed on the green diamond unfolding before me, that I never saw him coming until he landed on top of me.

He was leaning over me with this goofy grin, his beard nearly touching my chin and his banjo pointed at me like a machine gun. I did what any self-respecting eight-year-old would do in such a situation: I screamed as loud and as long as I could. My mother and her siblings were there in an instant and correctly sized up the harmlessness of the situation. My Uncle Jim helped me up, and then he, my mom, my Aunt Rose and my Uncle Bernard had a good laugh at my expense. Me? I couldn't take my eyes off of this hairy lunatic. If I allowed myself one unguarded moment, I was convinced he would snatch me. He'd tie a leash around me, and I would become his circus monkey.

I clung to my mother until the beard with the banjo disappeared. But I knew he was there, somewhere in that great expanse of a ballpark. One moment he was up on the third deck entertaining section 315, and then in an instant he was dancing on the roof of the visitor's dugout. If I blinked he'd be standing right in front of me again. So I didn't blink.

Only when the banjo man was out of my view could I watch the game. From our right field perch I was able to enjoy for the first time the cocky, surefooted trot of Reggie Jackson as he chased down and caught a deep fly on the run. I got to witness for the first time Campy Campaneris' menacing crouch at the plate daring the pitcher to sneak one past him. I observed Captain Sal Bando's blue-collar work ethic lived out at third base. I was there as Denny McLain notched his eighteenth victory on his way to an amazing 31-win season. It was like opening one present after another, each one more amazing and awe-inspiring than the last. On that July evening, however, most of my energies were focused on watching out for the caped phantom.

❀ ❀ ❀ ❀ ❀ ❀ ❀

It was as if a phantom was stalking the whole nation that year as well. 1968 was a tough year. Martin Luther King, Jr. had been silenced by the assassin's bullet. I remember standing outside on our front porch that April looking out onto our street simmering in an unnatural silence and wondering to myself if the world had gone a little crazy. I remember being awakened by my mother in the middle of the night that June. She was visibly shaken and in tears. She had roused all of us to tell us that Bobby Kennedy had been shot. There was the war in Vietnam going at full throttle, and the protesters camping out at People's Park in downtown Berkeley stopped traffic and burned

The graceful language of baseball muted all the vitriol, and its grit and grace transcended all the ugliness.

flags and raised the blood pressure of the nation. There were race riots and labor strikes and daily body counts. I honestly don't know how my parents were able to keep it together. That summer I think they mostly took their kids to the ballpark. There it didn't matter if you were a Democrat or Republican, black or white, man or woman, adult or child. The graceful language of baseball muted all the vitriol, and its grit and grace transcended all the ugliness.

For a few hours on a summer's weeknight or weekend, you got to loosen just a little the grip that fear had on you. You could get into a heated argument with a stranger sitting next to you in the bleachers and not worry that it would end in fisticuffs. You argued over a blown call at third or the idiotic move on the manager's part to yank his starting pitcher or the price of beer. And then Rick Monday or Danny Cater would park one in the left field bleachers and everyone would be hugging each other and slapping five and cheering the home team. There was an adrenaline rush, a surge of hope, and for a while we got to enjoy and celebrate what is best about us as human beings. Tomorrow's headlines would be tomorrow's headlines. For that moment, it was enough to be carried by the tide of simple human joy.

✤ ✤ ✤ ✤ ✤ ✤ ✤

I think it might have been during the seventh inning. McLain was working on his shutout and the vendors were racing up and down the aisles barking and begging and selling their wares. From what I remember, it began with a peanut. Someone a few rows up had tossed a peanut in the air, and it landed on the head of someone a few rows down from us. We were right in the middle. I remember having this eerie sense that someone had turned the thermostat up. It must have been the immediate tension created by the first peanut, then the angry, irritated glance up and back to see who had thrown it, then a guffaw and giggle and an "Ah, shut up and turn around, you stupid niggers."

I was eight years old, and though I had heard of the "N" word, I had never actually heard it spoken. Hearing it for the first time was like getting slapped across the face—with a shovel. I could only imagine what the black kids below us were thinking and feeling.

Then came another peanut. And another. And another.

It was raining peanuts. Above us was a collection of ten or twelve white guys in their twenties. They seemed thoroughly pleased with themselves. Below us were four or five black kids of high school age. The growing anger—and danger—in the situation was palpable, as it became quickly apparent that we were about to have a race riot on our hands.

As I look back on it now, I would have hoped that all the adults around us would have stepped up and diffused the situation. But that didn't happen. Most folks—my mom and her brothers and sister in-cluded—were caught off guard. Their first reaction was much like mine: mouths wide open in disbelief. But there were others, more than a few, who actually were enjoying the unfolding drama, seeing it, tragically, as a comedy, mimicking those who, for some God-forsaken reason, egg on the one on the window ledge with "Jump! Jump!"

I'd like to be able to say that there was no fight—that calmer heads prevailed—but that wouldn't be true. Punches were thrown. Blood was spilt. I was terrified, because the fighting converged on those of us un-lucky enough to be in the middle. It was nasty and it was visceral. The phantom of fear wrapped its clammy fingers around our necks once more. But it could have been much worse.

At first I could barely hear the cheerful, buoyant picking of the banjo. But it grew louder and stronger and more insistent. The lunatic with the beard was upon us before the security guards, and his eyes were wild and sad and cast in a light of urgency. Cheer-ing erupted all around us to welcome this holy minstrel, who cut a farcical, ridiculous pose with his cape and long

Cheering erupted all around us

to welcome this holy minstrel,

who cut a farcical, ridiculous pose

with his cape and long beard

but came armed for battle.

beard but came armed for battle. He played his banjo like I have never seen anyone play a musical instrument since. People started clapping and stomping to the beat, and that gave him the strength and courage to play on.

Slowly, one fighter, then another, then another looked up, punches halted in mid-release like in some Road Runner cartoon. Within half a minute, the warring factions disentangled and disengaged. Arms were grabbed, breaths were caught, steps were taken back from the edge, and a modicum of dignity and decency was restored. By the time banjo-man was finished picking and strumming, sweat was rolling down his forehead and cheeks and collecting on his beard. The entire section of the park erupted in a sustained ovation that seemed to me to shake the very heavens. The man with the banjo took a bow, and then started a cheer, "Let's go A's! Let's go A's! Let's go A's!" And within a minute the whole stadium reverberated with the echo of a new battle cry. Division had been routed; unity had been restored—at least for that one night.

❀ ❀ ❀ ❀ ❀ ❀ ❀

For me, the events of that game, from the moment I collided with the banjo player to that thunderous cheer, left me in a state of transfigured awe. It had been the wildest experience of my short life. Kafka wrote about having been filled once with a sense of endless astonishment at simply seeing a group of people cheerfully assembled. As I leaned against the railing looking out onto the Coliseum later that night, having witnessed both the grace and the gravity of the human condition, that partisan cheer washed over me like the waters of baptism, initiating me into a community of faith whose bible was baseball. I realized that I now belonged to a family built on loyalty and faith, a family that lived and died for The Game, and didn't care what else you believed in or did outside of it.

So it should come as no surprise to anyone that I see the Oakland Coliseum as a kind of cathedral, yet one more sacred place on the planet where I can encounter God. I did that night in July when I found myself in the right field bleachers of the cathedral on Heggenberger for the first time and felt the clamp of fear around my neck. God came to me that night in a long red beard wearing a cape and playing a banjo, and the din of human ugliness surrendered—as it always must—to the joyful music of grace and peace.

III.
Pinned by God

In his autobiography, the writer Nikos Kazantzakis writes of a time when he visited a monastery on Mount Athos in Greece as a young man. In one memorable interview he engaged an old monk who had a reputation for holiness. He asked the monk, "Do you still struggle with the devil?"

"Oh, no," the old man replied, "I used to struggle with him, when I was young, but now I've grown old and tired and the devil has grown old and tired with me. We leave each other alone!"

"So it's easier for you now?" asked the young Kazantzakis.

"Oh no," replied the old man. "It's worse, far worse! Now I wrestle with God!"

"You wrestle with God," blurted the surprised Kazantzakis, "and hope to win?"

"No," replied the old monk, "I wrestle with God and hope to lose!"

❀❀❀❀❀❀❀

I first came to know Giulio Orlando when he showed up for my American Literature class in his junior year of high school. His reputation as a bit of a rascal preceded him. And apparently his mom was drop-dead gorgeous, which his classmates at Notre Dame High School for Boys in Niles, Illinois, never let him forget. When I read the roll that day and noticed Giulio's name, I looked up and took note of his solid frame sitting there toward the back of the classroom, next to the likes of Chris Amatore, Vito Battista, Tony LaPalermo, and others whose surnames seemed to have been lifted from the rolls of the Cosa Nostra. Giulio seemed relatively harmless, I thought to myself at the time.

In fact he was a great kid, guileless and gregarious. I took hidden pleasure in seeing him trying to insinuate himself into my life as if we were great friends and close confidantes. Typically, he would enter the classroom each day and greet me with a boisterous "Hi ya, Fadder!" He would place his broad arm on my shoulder and survey the classroom as if we were going to team-teach that day.

"Mr. Orlando, you may take your seat," I would say, and he would saunter down the aisle with a big grin on his face. He was a bear of a boy with the heart of a child, and I looked forward to seeing him every day. There was a bit of the rapscallion in him though, as he was always on the lookout for ways to lighten the occasional (in my class at least) tedium with levity.

One afternoon, for instance, I was leading a discussion on some dead poet, and Giulio, bored beyond belief, took out his bottle of bubble liquid and started blowing bubbles with the accompanying wand. Scores of bubbles and subsequent laughter filled the back of the classroom before I could react.

"Mr. Orlando, please go to the Dean's Office."

"But, Father," Giulio responded with a sincere look on his face, "I'm only having a little fun wit' chew." I had to send him to the dean, of course, but secretly I didn't mind the bubbles at all. Whichever poet we were discussing would probably have delighted in Giulio's free-spirited antics.

Giulio was an easily distracted fellow, and his classmates took full advantage. One afternoon class in particular stands out among many. I had my back to the class as I was writing something on the board, when, out of nowhere, Giulio erupted. "Shut your mouth, you big, fat guinea!" I turned around to see Giulio, red-faced and ready to pounce on Chris Amatore, who was sitting to his right. I learned later that Chris, along with all the other guys surrounding Giulio, kept whispering Giulio's mother's name or his girlfriend's name—I can't remember which—bringing Giulio to a full boil.

"Mr. Orlando, please go to the Dean's Office."

"But Fadder," Giulio said, "don't dese other guys hafta go too? Amatore, you better shut your dago mouth!" Chris' head was almost between his legs as he tried to stifle his laughter, all the while apparently whispering the name over and over. I exercised my option not to send anyone to the dean this time, brought the class to quick order, and used the episode as a teachable moment in ethnic sensitivity. Amatore and the rest of the class were not offended by Giulio's crass ethnic slurs, but I made it clear that if I ever heard those words or any like them again, there would be hell to pay.

That entire year, Giulio became for me a mirror of humanity that I found both endearing and compelling. He was impetuous and brash, to be sure. He could be exasperating at times, but there was genuine goodness in him that could not be denied. He was flawed and forgivable—qualities that have been with our species since we got kicked out of the Garden of Eden.

Once, when reading through the letters of the writer Flannery O'Connor, I was at first startled by her articulation of the central Christian mystery that human life "has, for all its horror, been found by God to be worth dying for." For some reason, I immediately thought of the likes of Giulio Orlando

It dawned on me that O'Connor was right in her assessment of God and of us. We are worth dying for.

and Chris Amatore and their cohorts in crime, and it dawned on me that O'Connor was right in her assessment of God and of us. We are worth dying for.

❀ ❀ ❀ ❀ ❀ ❀ ❀

In February of Giulio's senior year, Notre Dame High School hosted the Illinois High School Wrestling Regional Tournament. Giulio, being in the highest weight class, was the last to wrestle that afternoon. He had reached the finals in quick order, dispatching one opponent after another with relative ease. To get to the final match, however, he had beaten the top-ranked state wrestler from powerhouse New Trier High School. All along, it was hilarious watching Giulio nervously pace and prowl the outskirts of the wrestling mats in the school gym between his matches; and when his name was announced for the championship match, he did what he always did: he ran over to the nearest garbage can and threw up. After that, he was good to go.

The final match of the tournament pitted Giulio against a corn-fed scrapper from Maine South High School. The thousand or so spectators in the stands, as well as all the competing wrestlers, focused their attention on the impending epic battle. Giulio, it seemed, was going to be the underdog. Just about everyone he wrestled was twenty, thirty pound heavier than he, including his final opponent

The referee brought the two together to shake hands, and with a whistle blow they began to wrestle. They moved slowly around the mat at first, each one training his eyes on the other. With bodies crouched and arms extended, they stalked each other and waited for an opening to exploit. After ten seconds or so, the battle was engaged as the two became locked in what seemed to be mortal combat. As we all watched, it became a living, breathing answer to the question: what happens when an immoveable object meets an irresistible force?

Muscles I suspect neither knew they had were enlisted in what quickly became a heroic battle of wills as well as brawn. Giulio was putting up a fight. The cheering was deafening as everyone realized that this was going to be a match long remembered. At one point early on, the wrestler from Maine South had Giulio on his back. If he could pin Giulio's shoulders to the mat for two seconds, the victory would be his. Giulio kept rocking his shoulders back and forth, fending off defeat as the referee, splayed on the mat and his head tucked into the wrestlers' shadows, waited patiently for Giulio's shoulder blades to surrender so he could call the match. It never happened.

Regulation time ended with the score tied. Giulio was pumped. Later he told me that he had been absolutely exhausted, but you wouldn't have known that by looking at him. His opponent carried himself with equal determination.

The overtime period began, and again the two stalked each other before their bodies locked. It seemed as if the kid from Maine South had the upper hand. Three or four times it looked as if he were going to take Giulio down, and each time Giulio managed to wriggle his way out. And then, at one point late in the match, it happened. Giulio had his opponent at the edge of the mat in a headlock. The cheering in the gym was deafening as the clock continued to wind down. In one last surge of energy, Giulio literally lifted his opponent off the ground—the guy had to have weighed over two hundred and fifty pounds—and slammed him to the ground, and the referee raised his hand with two fingers showing. With time ticking down to zero, Giulio had taken a two-point lead. The gym descended into near-chaos as it began to dawn on everyone that Giulio was going to win.

We've got to be careful.

If we give God the slightest opening,

he's going to pounce.

He's going to pin us too.

The wrestler from Maine South fought back with the last ounce of energy he had, but Giulio would not to be denied. The buzzer screamed, and Giulio jumped up from the mat victorious. When the referee raised Giulio's hand in triumph a moment later, I realized that I had been a witness to an event that transcended wrestling.

❋ ❋ ❋ ❋ ❋ ❋

Someone once asked me why the Holy Spirit is often depicted as fire. I think it has to do with the heart of God and the fire that burns eternally within it. Indeed, I am convinced God has the burning heart of a wrestler. We've got to be careful. If we give God the slightest opening, he's going to pounce. He's going to pin us too.

FIVE

Holy Matrimony: Union and Unity

The voice of my beloved!
Look, he comes
leaping upon the mountains,
bounding over the hills.
My lover is like a gazelle or a young stag.
Look, there he stands behind our wall,
gazing in at the windows,
looking through the lattice.
My beloved speaks and says to me,
"Arise, my love, my fair one, and come away....
O my dove, in the clefts of the rock,
in the covert of the cliff,
let me see your face,
let me hear your voice;
for your voice is sweet,
and your face is lovely...."
Set me as a seal upon your heart,
as a seal upon your arm;
for love is strong as death,
passion fierce as the grave.
Its flashes are flashes of fire, a raging flame.
Many waters cannot quench love,
Neither can floods drown it."

Song of Songs 2:8-10, 14; 8:6-7

I.
"Isn't This Beautiful!"

Mom and Dad would be so pleased. All of their children found someone to love and marry; and I, a Holy Cross priest, found a community of men who inspired me to hitch my wagon to theirs. One day at the Basilica of Sacred Heart at Notre Dame I made *my* vows to God forever—to living a life of poverty, chastity, and obedience. Mom was there along with all my brothers and sisters and their spouses. Many of them were in tears. They already knew what I was getting myself into even if I didn't, this vowed life that mercifully whittles down the ego and exposes every human imperfection and dares you to surrender to love anyway. Making a vow is the easy part. Living the vow faithfully requires intestinal and spiritual fortitude.

The sun comes up in the east, and married folk everywhere roll over in their beds and look at their still-sleeping spouses with their loose-skinned chicken necks and puffy eyes, their double chins and healthy paunches and bald patches, and sometimes they whimper. But at some appointed moment in that morning—while scrubbing off morning muck in the shower or sipping the first cup of coffee or dropping the kids off at school—husbands and wives sign up for another day of fidelity. It takes guts to live the vowed life.

❀ ❀ ❀ ❀ ❀ ❀

A couple of years ago an elderly couple, accompanied by their children and grandchildren, arrived at the Saturday evening Mass to renew their vows on their sixtieth wedding anniversary. Lorene and Ches held hands as they stood facing each other. My hunch was that their sixty years had gone by rather quickly, and I asked them if this was true. Ches smiled and said loud enough for everyone to hear, "Father, my bride is more beautiful now than she was the day we were married." He said this with conviction. Ches was speaking the truth and we all knew it. Lorene blushed, of course, but she too knew it was true.

Sixty years of loving had smoothed out the wrinkles and straightened the curving spines and erased the age spots. Beauty had been liberated from the chains and shackles of dusty time. We all got a glimpse of the infinite horizon that night, and I have to tell you that it was an awesome sight. There is something of the eternal in vowed love that makes me think no one should be able to leave the planet without having touched it, tasted it, smelled it, seen it, heard it, and lived it.

❖ ❖ ❖ ❖ ❖ ❖

I have another story of fidelity and unity, one that is much like Ches and Lorene's. I first met Tracie and Lori at my sister Julie's workplace. They all worked for the public defender's office in downtown Portland. Julie and Tracie were attorneys and Lori was an investigator. Occasionally we would get together for a lunch or a weekend softball game. I wasn't at all surprised then to see them at my sister Julie's wedding to her husband Greg that summer of 1994 along with many of their colleagues.

We all got a glimpse of the infinite horizon that night, and I have to tell you that it was an awesome sight.

A couple of months later Tracie and Lori called and asked if we could get together. We met in my office at the Downtown Chapel where I was working at the time. The two young women told me how much they loved Julie and Greg's wedding, how joyful and hopeful it was. (It had been moving for all of us, myself included, because it was the first family celebration after our Mom's death, so the Hannon clan had been determined to make it a wedding everyone would remember.) I can still see Julie walking down the aisle on the arm of our brother Greg. Seeing them holding onto each other for dear life filled everyone with teary joy, including Tracie and Lori.

Now they were the couple who sat before me holding hands, asking if I would witness *their* marriage. I had never been faced with this situation before. They were planning to exchange vows in the spring in the back yard of Lori's parents home and wanted me to be there to witness it. I was, after all, their priest.

We spent the evening talking this over. I told them that I could not perform a wedding celebration for them, given the Church's teaching on gay marriage. We mulled over various options of how I might participate. I asked them if anyone would be scandalized by my presence. They both responded strongly that both of their families and all of their friends supported their decision.

This is what we came up with. I would prepare them for marriage as I would prepare any other couple. This involved them meeting me regularly for counseling, attending an engaged couple's retreat, and taking the pre-marriage inventory most dioceses use with engaged couples. I would attend the wedding in a suit and tie and offer them a blessing, but I would not "officiate." They happily agreed to this arrangement; and so for the next six months we spent time together, and I helped them prepare for the day they would exchange their vows of love and fidelity.

The day arrived. Tracie's parents and siblings were all there along with Lori's expansive Irish-Catholic family. Including their close friends, we numbered seventy or eighty men, women, and children. The day was made all the more poignant by the presence of Lori's dad, who was very ill. He was determined to make it to that day, and he did. When he came out to the back yard right before the ceremony began, Lori burst into tears.

Tracie and Lori promised to love each other for the rest of their lives. They kissed and everyone who had cameras snapped photographs. I came forward and asked the God of Love to bless them with a love stronger than death. Everyone cheered. With that, the celebration began.

❀ ❀ ❀ ❀ ❀ ❀

A few weeks later Lori called me. She asked if I might come over to her parent's home. Her dad was near death and wanted to be anointed. I grabbed my oils and headed over immediately.

Lori and Tracie greeted me at the door and we exchanged hugs. Lori, the baby of her family, seemed particularly fragile as it began to dawn on her that her father was going to die. Tracie held her. I walked with them to the living room, where Lori's father was sitting in his favorite recliner. There he was, a mere shadow of the stocky, muscled fellow he must have been in his prime—a tavern owner, a husband, father of many, and grandfather to dozens. His family was all there surrounding him, twenty-five or more of them.

I went up to the dying man and shook his hand. "Ah, Father Pat," he said, "Thanks so much for coming by. I hope it's not too much of a bother."

"Are you kidding me?" I said with a sad laugh. "I can't imagine wanting to be anywhere else right now."

I invited everyone to gather closely together and I placed my purple stole over my shoulders. We began to pray for Lori's dad. All the while, he sat there with his eyes wide open in wonder. Before I anointed his forehead and the palms of his hands, I laid my hands on his head and prayed for him, as the Sacrament of the Anointing of the Sick requires. Then, as is my custom, I invited everyone to come forward, lay their hands on his head one at a time, and offer a silent blessing. And so they lined up. Lori's mom went first, then the couple's children and their spouses, and finally their grandchildren. Delicate hands, calloused hands, tiny hands, bony hands: they came bearing holy prayers of promise and hope and enduring, tear-drenched love. Among them were Lori and her spouse, Tracie.

The entire time, Lori's father kept repeating the same words, "Isn't this beautiful! Isn't this beautiful!" It was a moment of truth and a welcomed glimpse of the infinite horizon for all of us. Later that evening, Lori's mother tucked her tiny frame into the empty space in that recliner and held her husband's head in her arms. She kissed his forehead and stroked his hair and told him how much she loved him. I am quite sure that he died in her arms.

It is beautiful, indeed, this life that we have been gifted with. There is something of the eternal in vowed love that makes me think no one should be able to leave the planet without having touched it, tasted it, smelled it, seen it, heard it, and lived it.

II.
Tying the Knot

My education into matters of Christian marriage began at a very early age. I was probably five or six when it began to dawn on me that Mom and Dad had a relationship unique unto themselves. As far as I could tell before then, their existence had begun with me, or at least with my eldest sibling.

It had never occurred to me that at some point my parents had fallen madly in love and so wedded their hearts together that you could not tell where one of them ended and the other began. I knew they slept together in the same bed, but this was not particularly revelatory to a kid. I slept in the same bed with my brother Greg for ten years of my life. Quite frankly, there wasn't a whole lot of loving go on. Those days I often approached bedtime with great trepidation, for most nights the last words spoken between Greg and me went something like this:

"Pat?"

"Yeah?"

"I just wanted to tell you that sometime tonight—I'm not saying when—but sometime tonight I'm going to get you. Good night."

Greg and I fought over covers, kicked each other until our bodies were blue with bruises, and generally treated the other as an unwelcome guest at a party. For a couple of years we slept in bunk beds. Those were the most restful, relaxing nights of my childhood. When watching an episode of *I Love Lucy* about that time, I understood perfectly why Lucy and Ricky slept in separate beds, and I wondered why my parents had not yet seen the light.

❈ ❈ ❈ ❈ ❈ ❈

One night, however, my father taught me an important lesson about the matrimonial bond, a lesson about married love I would only come to cherish all the more when it was eclipsed by the shadow of my parents' deaths.

To appreciate the events of that particular night more fully, it might be helpful to know that when my family moved out of our home on Arcadian Drive we had to replace every door in the house. They were pock-marked with dents and holes, evidence of their practical purpose as the defense of last resort from thrown shoes and fists and books and garden tools.

We were a rambunctious tribe of children, with serious territorial issues. Give us a Zen Buddhist monk for one week back then, and we would have reduced him to a quivering, twitching wreck with dark, foreboding thoughts. In the fifteen hundred square feet of our domestic abode there was only one place any of us kids could find a moment's peace: the bathroom. We used to camp out in the bathroom. I give credit to those private moments for my love of reading. I never went to the bathroom without a book or magazine in hand.

Maybe this tendency to hog is why Mom eventually took the doorknob off that bathroom door. But with that knob went any hope for a moment's solitude in our home. We were thereafter sentenced to a life of unabated rubbed shoulders, clenched fists, and sibling bellicosity. Mom became the de facto referee: resolving disputes, handing down sentences that mostly fit the crimes, and issuing tickets-of-leave when we gained parole. Up until that night—by my recollection—Dad had never entered into the disiplinary fray. Given his job as an attorney, this was rather ironic. I could have benefited from his representation (or at least his counsel) on a number of occasions back then.

We were in our room that night, my brothers Greg and Mike and me. It had begun innocuously enough. Greg and Mike were wrestling playfully. Laughter filled the room; but a punch that was just a *little* too

Give us a Zen Buddhist monk

for one week back then,

and we would have reduced him

to a quivering, twitching wreck

with dark, foreboding thoughts.

hard or an elbow to the ribs that was just a *tad* menacing changed the tenor of the match, and it devolved into a fight to the death between the two of them. At some point I jumped into the fray, probably for the pure sport of it.

Before any of us could stop, we were all red-eared, flush-faced, and determined—each of us trying to exact his pound of flesh from the other two. Mom arrived at our door with her patented look of consternation, and we were duly sentenced to our beds where, by God, we were to stay, or, by God, if we didn't, there would be hell to pay.

Two minutes—maybe—elapsed before Mike and Greg were at it again. Clearly they feared neither God nor Mom. I stayed put in my bed because something told me that this was going to turn out badly, which it did. Mom came to the room a second time and tried to establish order, but this time she was met with snickering from my two brothers. I lay perfectly still, stunned by this act of filial rebellion. Mom stood there for a moment, flummoxed by the fact that two of her children had, for all intents and purposes, mutinied. She was, I think, reduced and humiliated by the experience. She started to leave, but when she reached the door she turned back toward us and burst into tears. Then she left, her shoulders slumped, defeated by her children for the first time in her maternal career. Greg and Mike didn't say a word, and I…well, I cried. None of us could go to sleep.

❖ ❖ ❖ ❖ ❖ ❖ ❖

It was an hour or so later that Dad walked down the stairs and came to our room. It was as if he wanted to sneak up on us. I knew it was Dad though. I had the ears of a young buck. The moment of reckoning had arrived. With only seconds to spare, I darted to the closet and dove inside, shutting the door behind me. Mike and Greg never knew what hit them. From what I could tell, they had tried to hide under the covers. Did they honestly think that thin cotton sheets and polyester-blended blankets could save them?

As Mike and Greg were being punished, I sat in the darkness of the closet, counting my lucky stars. I heard my brothers yelping and crying, and I drew secret satisfaction from the fact that there was justice in the universe after all. After a moment, an eerie calm seemed to descend upon the room. Had Dad left? I wasn't sure, so I continued to stay in the closet.

Then a shadow appeared at the bottom of the door where a thin slice of light came through. The door slowly opened. It was Dad. He was still holding the strap of his belt in his hand. He had the strangest look on his face. He was angry, for sure, but there was this look of devastation on his face as well. He had been crying. It was as if someone had wounded him in a way that would never go away.

"Dad!" I cried, "I didn't do *anything*!"

"You're right, Son," he said. "You didn't *do* a damn thing."

And then he whipped my little behind.

❄ ❄ ❄ ❄ ❄ ❄ ❄

That was the first and, to my knowledge, the only time that Dad ever took a belt to one of his kids. In hurting Mom, we had hurt Dad. It was that simple. I realized this years after the fact, when I was old enough to understand that Dad was first and foremost—before he was a father, or a lawyer, or a Catholic, or a Republican, or even a man—a husband who had given himself to his wife in a way only spouses can do. When he and Monica tied that knot, nothing was ever going to untie it. They were, literally, one flesh.

The first Christmas after our father's death, all of us were gathered in the living room with Mom. The presents had all been unwrapped. Mom went to her bedroom for a moment and returned with a stack of letters, fourteen of them. They were the love letters Dad had written in his near-illegible, southpaw cursive to Mom when they

It was a mystical experience to get a peek at the love that had so filled our parents that it created us.

were courting. She allowed us to read them for the first time. They revealed a passionate love affair between a young man and a young woman who were frustrated by the miles that separated them. They spoke of an enduring love that confounds the limits of time and space and the fragility of the human heart.

My siblings and I sat there in awe as Mom gave us a glimpse of our dad as her lover and best friend. We passed the letters around and read them in turn, laughing and crying. It was a mystical experience to get a peek at the love that had so filled our parents that it created us.

One letter, written a year before their marriage, ended this way:

Well, darling, it's 2:30 and I had better start to work. Keep writing those letters, for they are the only thing I have to look forward to at night. It sure is wonderful knowing that you are in love with me, even though you couldn't be as much in love as I am. I think of you all the time, Monica—wondering what you are doing, worrying if you love me as much as ever, and wishing I had you with me for at least a little while. I love you, Bill.

I wish my brothers and I had understood this relationship that awful night when we made our father hit us to protect the love of his life. We would have been more respectful of our mother, and of him. That's for sure.

III.
Nighttime in a Tree Fort with My Friends

When I was a young boy and gainfully employed as a paperboy for the Oakland *Tribune*, I used to wile away the summer days with two other paperboys, Steve and Michael. Steve was the man of his house; his dad had left him and his younger brothers and sisters and his mother when he was a boy. Steve and his family were practicing Mormons and thus an endless source of fascination to me. Michael was a black kid who grew up in Oakland before his family moved to my hometown. Michael was a bible-thumping Baptist; and so he, too, captivated me with his ability to quote chapter and verse from books of the Bible I had barely heard of.

I, of course, was the Catholic of the triumvirate and an endless source of fascination to them. I'm sure they thought I was one of those Catholics with a scapular dangling from my neck and a picture of the pope hanging over the kitchen sink. They probably thought I had one of those mothers who wore rosary beads around her hand as she stirred the pot of morning mush, chatted on the phone, or vacuumed the living room carpet. What they suggested about my mother was partially true. She was a living, breathing saint: her patience and fortitude in the face of nine overactive children was legendary in our neighborhood; but she could also cuss and scream and raise holy hell with the best of the heathens when she had to.

A cradle Catholic, I never missed Sunday Mass as a kid. I went to parochial school and said grace before supper with the rest of the tribe (a blessing supplemented with a Hail Mary—a family tradition), but that was about the extent of my Catholicity. I was an altar boy, too, which might at first blush reflect more religious piety than I actually deserved. My older brothers drafted me into liturgical service so that I could cover for them at early Sunday Masses when they were too tired to get out of bed. The great draw to serving Mass for me, to tell the truth, was that altar boys got out of class an awful lot during the school week for funerals.

A Latter-Day Saint, a Southern Baptist, and a Roman Catholic: you would have thought that the deep chasm of religious difference would have kept us at a suspicious distance, but that was never the case. For even though we went to different churches on Sundays, found our confidence and conviction from different creeds, and generally held fast to seemingly separate spiritual paths, the rest of the week we treated each other like brothers. Years later when I first read the words of the Irish poet Patrick Kavanagh, that "God is found in the bits and pieces of Everyday, a kiss here and a laugh again, and sometimes tears, a pearl necklace round the neck of poverty," I thought of those idyllic summers with Steve and Michael and began to understand what it was that bound us to such brotherhood. It was our poverty, pure and simple.

❈ ❈ ❈ ❈ ❈ ❈ ❈

Clearly the three of us never went hungry for very long. Each of us had a bed to sleep in at night and blankets to shield us from the cold. We ploughed through our textbooks at school with the rest of our juvenile tribe. We were not destitute; but we were poor. Each of us came from large families on tight budgets, so we knew that whatever treasure came our way usually had the fingerprints of older siblings all over them, or in Steve's case, the fingerprints of generous strangers. We rarely spent our paper route money, because our monthly receipts were quickly squirreled away by our parents into savings accounts earmarked for college, cars, and the women we would one day call our wives, should they have us.

But there were pearls that "draped the neck" of our poverty. It became our summertime morning ritual when we met at first light at the tree fort in the hills behind Steve's house to empty our pockets and to see what resources we had for the day. Though it never added up to much, by sundown, when we retired once more back to that old oak, it seemed we had always managed to spend the day as kings and princes, exhausted by our exploits, warmed by our laughter, and inspired by newly hatched plots that we would spring on the world the next day. With barely anything to our names, we would have dined on soda pop and maple bars, bowled a game or two at the bowling alley, or taken a round trip bus ride into downtown Oakland or San Francisco.

We were content in our relative poverty because it seemed necessary for our happiness. We were aware of the rich kid down the street from Steve's house who owned four pairs of tennis shoes and rode a five-speed and vacationed at Lake Tahoe with his family. We knew the family down the street from my house that owned a speedboat and spent sunny Saturdays water-skiing up at Lake Barryessa. We knew families who had maids and cooks, lawn service, and milk delivered to their doorsteps. We never begrudged them of such luxuries, but we were also convinced that they weren't having nearly as much fun as we were having.

It seemed we had always managed to spend the day as kings and princes, exhausted by our exploits, warmed by our laughter, and inspired by newly hatched plots that we would spring on the world the next day.

Staying up late at night in our tree fort, we spoke every so often of one day vacationing at Lake Tahoe or skiing at Lake Barryessa or having an army of maids, but that was the stuff of dreams. Most nights we tended to the business of the moment: drawing deep satisfaction from the brotherhood nurtured every morning when we emptied our threadbare pockets and every night when we marveled at what we had done with next to nothing.

❋ ❋ ❋ ❋ ❋ ❋

One summer afternoon, while we were lollygagging through some neighborhood in San Francisco, Michael stumbled upon what turned out to be the most amazing prize any of us had ever captured. Steve and

I were waiting for hot dogs and sodas at the outside pick-up window of a refreshment stand when we heard Michael yelling for us as he raced down the street past us. We thought he had done something danger-ously wicked, so we bolted down the street after him, leaving our unpaid-for food order behind us. We ran for what seemed a mile when we all stopped to catch our breath.

"Look," Michael gasped between gulps of breath, "what I found on the sidewalk!" He dug into his pocket and retrieved a fifty-dollar bill. At first we thought it was a fake. I don't think any of us had ever seen a fifty-dollar bill before; but we inspected it like treasury agents, and it passed muster. Suddenly, the three of us were rich beyond our wildest dreams, because it never occurred to any of us that a) the money belonged to someone else who might be looking for it, or b) the money belonged to Michael because he had found it, or c) even if it was ours, we shouldn't spend it all right away.

Instead, we hightailed it back to the East Bay and went to an Oak-land A's game. We sat in the bleachers and ate hotdogs and guzzled Cokes until we were sure our bellies were going to burst. We bought pennants and baseball cards and souvenir programs—inside the ballpark! Then we dined on double cheeseburgers and chocolate malts at Sil's on Foothill Boulevard and caught a movie at the Chabot Theatre on Castro Valley Boulevard.

By the time we retreated to our tree fort it was well past sundown. We lit candles and sat on the edge of the wooden platform that jutted out into the darkness. Steve replaced the batteries in the old radio we had, and immediately we were serenaded by a sultry voice that made us melt; maybe it was Linda Ronstadt or Mama Cass, I don't remember. Looking out onto the valley of lights below, it felt as if we had been transported to the top of the world. Steve, Michael, and I sat there in silence, breath-ing deeply, each of us no doubt attuned to the purring of our individual hearts.

We began that day in hushed whispers, and by nightfall a chorus of crickets serenaded us under a canopy of twinkling lights. That peaceful silence was a benediction, a blessing from the Creator who had made it all possible: the fifty-dollar bill, the wood and nails that constituted the bleachers at the Oakland Coliseum, the baseballs and bats, the cows that made the hot dogs and cheeseburgers and the milk shakes. It was a blessing from the one who gave us the wax and wick that gave us light that night and the cricket chorus and the breath that we needed to laugh and cheer and, in the end, sigh with utter contentment.

It was all gift, graciously and wonderfully and mysteriously given, and humbly received.

SIX

Holy Orders: Christ for Others

In the year that King Uzziah died,
I saw the Lord seated on a throne, high and lofty,
and the hem of his robe filled the temple.
Seraphs were in attendance above him;
each had six wings:
with two they covered their faces,
and with two they covered their feet,
and with two they flew.
And one called to another and said:
"Holy, holy, holy is the Lord of hosts;
the whole earth is full of his glory."
The pivots on the thresholds shook
at the voices of those who called,
and the house filled with smoke.
And I said, "Woe is me!
I am lost, for I am a man of unclean lips,
and I live among a people of unclean lips;
yet my eyes have seen the King, the Lord of hosts!"
Then one of the seraphs flew to me, holding a live coal
that had been taken from the altar with a pair of tongs.
The seraph touched my mouth with it and said:
"Now that this has touched your lips,
your guilt has departed and your sin is blotted out."
Then I heard the voice of the Lord saying,
"Whom shall I send, and who will go for us?"
And I said, "Here I am, send me!"

Isaiah 6:1-8

I.
Buck Up, Little Camper

It was only the first week of classes and I was ready to leave. I was an eighteen-year-old freshman at the University of Portland, and while it seemed that everyone else was adjusting just fine, I was sunk in desperation. I was away from home for the first time. I was lost. Hunkered down in my room one night on the phone with my mother, I told her that I should never have gone away to college.

"I want to come home," I said.

"Pat," she said, "go to sleep. You're going to be fine. Besides, you can't come home. I turned your bedroom into my sewing room."

❖ ❖ ❖ ❖ ❖ ❖

A few days later, I was on the phone again, this time with my brother Mike, whose turn it was to talk me off the ledge. He had graduated from the University of Portland earlier that spring. I had gotten my first exam back in Dr. Faller's Introduction to Philosophy class and was devastated by the failing grade I had received.

"Pat, don't worry. I failed that test too," he said, "and I ended up getting an A in the class." Years later, Mike told me he had lied to make me feel better. (It hadn't, but it did motivate me enough to get an A myself.)

Most of the time that first semester, I slept, ate, went to class, studied, and took solitary walks on the Bluff. I envied the students in my dorm who appeared unruffled by the change that was so obviously buffeting our lives and seemed to relish the opportunity to prove their mettle in an impossible situation.

I, on the other hand, was quietly planning my funeral. I'm not kidding. I used to spend time wondering who was going to show up, what they would say about me, and what suit Mom and Dad would dress me in. (I didn't own a suit at the time.)

I hated the gnawing, empty feeling in my gut I felt most mornings. I dreaded the desolate nights that sadly transmogrified a typical college day for me into a trip to the dentist. I realize now that I was suffering not only the normal emotional pains of separation anxiety but also the first of many episodes of melancholy that have haunted me my entire life. It is an experience that many college students have, but many of them don't know what is happening to them. I certainly didn't.

It is testimony to the human capacity to endure and even thrive in times of trial that I look back now on those first days of college with great affection and fondness. I recall professors who knew me be by name, classes that enthralled and captivated me, keggers on the Bluff, toga parties, and trips to the ocean beaches. Had I not crossed paths with a woman one late afternoon in downtown Portland, however, I might have given in to the darkness of my mind and returned home defeated, with my tail between my legs. The thought of that possibility gives me a cold chill even as I write these words.

✿ ✿ ✿ ✿ ✿ ✿ ✿

I was in an especially depressed mood the day I met the woman. I was fed up with myself and bored by the monotony of my self-pity. It was a typical late-fall Portland day, and I found a welcome companion in the rain and chill and gray cloud cover. I decided to take the bus downtown from campus and catch a movie by myself, but by the time I got there, the show I wanted to see had already started. So I just walked around town, with no destination in mind and no joy in my heart.

I was trying to talk myself out of the black mood that was overtaking my life. I told myself what a privileged place I had in the world. I was young, educated, and healthy. I had a mom and dad and brothers and sisters who loved me. I had friends. I had a warm place to sleep at night and three squares a day. *"Get over yourself!"* I practically yelled out loud.

But my self-therapy wasn't working. The troglodytic demons still lurked, luring me back to the comfort and safety of the family cave. Walking up a nearly-abandoned street, I could feel hope leaking out of me, and I remember thinking that I had been reduced to a mere spectator in my own life. I was seriously pissed that no one had ever told me this could happen, and I swear I was ready to pack it in.

God only knows what expression these dark thoughts painted on my face, but just then I saw a woman coming toward me. She had her eyes locked on me. I veered to the right so we could pass like the strangers we were, but then she veered to her left. I then tacked to my left, thinking to myself that the woman was probably drunk, but then she angled to her right. We were on a collision course, and she seemed hell-bent on making it happen.

Finally, I put my head down and walked straight ahead, hoping the woman would back down from this bizarre game of pedestrian "chicken," but she continued on a trajectory that could only collide with my own. Eventually we stopped, standing face-to-face with each other, only inches apart, in what for me was a moment of great awkwardness.

I could feel hope leaking out of me,

and I remember thinking

that I had been reduced

to a mere spectator in my own life.

For the woman, however, the encounter seemed to confirm some deep desire within her that our paths cross. It was as if it had been ordained that we were to meet. I looked up with vexation and saw the face of someone who had mustered as much poise and dignity as anyone could in such a situation. She smiled softly, searching for my soul behind my pale blue eyes and then apparently found what she was looking for. She touched my shoulder. "Buck up, little camper," she whispered to me. And then she continued on her way.

❀ ❀ ❀ ❀ ❀ ❀

That's it. That was the full extent of the encounter. I stood there for a few moments stunned. I remember saying to myself: *Don't forget this moment, Pat; it is important.*

It was. Since that chance meeting in a street over thirty years ago, I have endured many transitions far more painful and arduous than the one of my eighteenth year. I have walked the path of passage humbly with others as friend, counselor, brother, and priest: moments of death and divorce and disease and desperation and, yes, depression. Through all those moments of personal metamorphosis and times of walking with others as they traverse the cliffs of hell, I have never forgotten that woman who was determined to bump into a struggling college student in his desperate moment, knowing that she had something to give me expressed in a simple act of human kindness.

She was a priest to me at that moment, as I have tried to be a priest to others ever since.

II.
Bendix Woods

The first stirrings of a priestly vocation occurred when I was five or six. My brothers Mike and Jack were scheduled to serve morning Mass one summer day, and they let me tag along. One of them came up with the great idea of suiting me up for the game, and I was more than happy to oblige. I knew eventually I would follow my four older brothers as an altar server. Receiving a little on-the-job training couldn't hurt.

Everything went well until the time came for one of us to bring the cruets of wine and water to the altar during the Offertory. Mike handed me both cruets and pushed me toward Fr. Stack, who was waiting for me with growing impatience. Without further instruction I approached the pastor. Common sense told me that Fr. Stack wanted the wine poured into the chalice first, which I did. Upon emptying the entire cruet of wine, I proceeded to pour the water. After I had poured just a tad of water, Fr. Stack raised the chalice. I was later told that this was a non-verbal cue to cease the pouring. I, however, did not cease the pouring. In fact, as Fr. Stack's eyes grew large in stunned exasperation, I poured the entire cruet of water into the chalice. Those being the days in the Church when only the priest received from the cup, I had left Fr. Stack with a chalice filled nearly to the brim with heavily diluted altar wine. He was not pleased.

Returning to my brothers, who were now doubled over in pain as they tried to suppress their laughter, I sat down and looked back at Fr. Stack who had already moved on, whispering the priestly prayers with such reverence and concentration that it was as if he had been transported to a different dimension. So I did what I saw Fr. Stack do: I closed my eyes and prayed as one who aspires to be holy. Of course, I prayed that God would smite my brothers, a less-than-noble petition, I know, but you have to start somewhere.

❀ ❀ ❀ ❀ ❀ ❀

A year later, toward the end of my second year at Our Lady of Grace School, Sister Anna Maria, while cleaning out her closet in the back of the classroom, came upon a box of Catholic accoutrements—little plastic statues of saints, holy cards, rosaries—a veritable treasure-trove of religious kitsch. She unloaded as much as she could on us before stumbling upon a beautiful crucifix wrapped in thin tissue.

If I didn't put my hand down immediately, this would be grist for the mockery mill for years

"Oh, my," she said, as she peeled away the tissue wrapping. "Who here plans on becoming a priest?" Immediately my hand shot up. It was as close to an out-of-body-experience I have ever had. I was looking down on myself in a panic, in deference to the law of unintended consequences, knowing that if I didn't put my hand down immediately, this would be grist for the mockery mill for years to come as far as my classmates would be concerned.

"Patrick Hannon!" Sister Anna Maria said, loud enough for everyone in the class to hear, "I have a *special* gift for you." She motioned me over, and along the way, I could hear the boys snickering and licking their chops.

I am almost certain I got into a fight that very afternoon over the matter, but if it wasn't that afternoon, it was one soon after. "Father Pat" was what they called me for the next six years. Mostly I ignored them, but when they caught me on a bad day, I was all fist and fury.

One day in the seventh grade, for instance, I was shooting baskets during recess. Richard Steinberg, a kid who outweighed me by at least fifty pounds, approached with a sinister smile. "Hey, *Father*," he said. "Give me the basketball."

"Go to hell, Steinberg," I said without looking at him.

Richard approached me and promptly grabbed the ball from my hands. He began to walk away with it, bouncing it toward the far court. I had had enough. I walked steadily towards him, my ears bright red, my fists clenched. He probably was going to beat the tar out of me, but at least I would get a few licks in. I had to take a stand.

"*Steinberg,*" I shouted for everyone to hear, "*give me back the frickin' ball!*" But I didn't say "frickin." Richard turned around ready to beat me into next week, and then his face blanched. He very slowly handed me the basketball. Everyone was as stunned as I, and I secretly rejoiced that my salty language coupled with a bit of courage had won the day.

Turning around in triumph, I abruptly faced Fr. Stack standing three feet away. He didn't say a word. His eyebrows were lifted ever-so-slightly, but the event didn't seem to take him off stride as he recommenced his walk, thumbing his rosary beads.

I was scheduled to serve morning Mass the following day. As I was putting on my black cassock and white surplus in the back of the sacristy, Fr. Stack approached.

"Pat," he said very softly, "about yesterday." I couldn't even face him as he spoke, I was so ashamed.

"Let's not have that happen again," he said.

"Yes, Father," I said.

Though I wouldn't swear to it, I am confident I heard a faint chuckle as Fr. Stack made his way beyond my earshot.

❖ ❖ ❖ ❖ ❖ ❖ ❖

One wintry evening while I was studying at the Holy Cross Fathers' seminary at Notre Dame in Indiana, a dozen or so of my brother seminarians and I decided to go to Bendix Woods on the outskirts of South Bend for a night of snow tubing. A steep hill covered in several feet of snow provided the necessary slope on which we might risk life and limb in pursuit of a moderate adrenaline rush.

Dinky kids wrapped in coat and cap and scarf and mittens skedaddled up that hill with their little legs and huge eyes, their arms holding on to rubber innertubes three times their size; and without a moment's hesitation they reclined on their tubes, pushed off, and sailed down the hill at a chilling clip. They screamed all the way down, but there was a hint of holiness in their howling. Gravity gripped them on their inexorable journey, but in the absence of fear and self-consciousness they must have felt a divine swoop, a journey more inward than downward, to the very heart of existence.

After ten minutes of snow tubing, all of us seminarians had become children. We raced little boys and little girls to the top of the hill and jockeyed for position. We postured and preened and dared to one-up each other. And it wasn't just us. Honestly. I saw men and women twice my age, having stripped themselves of all pretension, acting like silly school children, lost in unfettered joy. It was a sight to behold.

In the absence of fear

and self-consciousness

they must have felt a divine swoop,

a journey more inward

than downward,

to the very heart of existence.

Toward the end of the evening, one in our group came up with the hair-brained idea of forming a phalanx of tubes onto which we all would pile. The heaviest of us would be positioned at the front to create maximum momentum and velocity. Word of our daring plan began to spread among snow tubers lining the hill, and more than a few adults near us counseled us to rethink the game plan, even as their children urged us on. I was on the second layer of bodies toward the back, along with the other lightweights. The bigger-boned were up front. With sober signs of the cross, we pushed off to the sound of young cherubs cheering and the isolated adult exclamatory prayer, "Oh, dear God!"

At first I thought we had miscalculated our weight distribution, because we weren't accelerating as fast as I thought we should have, but after twenty-five yards we began to pick up speed. It must have been an amazing sight seeing a dozen full-grown male adults piled onto each other, sailing down a snowy decline screaming and whooping it up. At one point I distinctly remember hearing a teenaged boy, a veteran of the slope no doubt, yell at us: "You're going too fast!" None of us was worried because we knew that at the end of the course there was an abrupt incline that would insure a safe terminus to the journey. (Think of those gravel turnoffs you often see on highways built for rigs that have lost their brakes and you have the basic concept.)

The problem, of which we all became aware simultaneously, was that as we neared the end of the course, we were still gaining speed. I might have had the best view as we approached the end. Picture the phalanx of rubber tubes and human bodies hitting a wall. See bodies go air bound, arms and legs akimbo. Witness bodies and rubber tubes bouncing several times before settling in the snow, a tangle of rubber and bruised flesh.

That might have been the happiest moment in my life up until then. We laughed until it hurt. I remember thinking then that *this* was the kind of community I wanted to be part of: men who could so easily surrender to joy, who weren't afraid to be silly when the circumstances called for it, who carried with them an image of a laughing Christ.

We stayed up long into the night and early morning, playing games in the recreation room of the seminary, bearing the happy wounds of a fully lived day. I stumbled to my bed at dawn. Before I went to sleep, I picked up Aelred of Rievaulx's meditation *Spiritual Friendship* and read a few pages. In it he wrote, "No medicine is more valuable, none more efficacious, none better suited to the cure of all our temporal ills than a friend to whom we may turn for consolation in time of trouble—and with whom we may share our happiness in time of joy."

In my years of priestly preparation, I was surrounded by priests who reminded me of my old pastor, a human and holy man who could so easily surrender to joy, who could lose himself in prayer, who told me early on in life that if you want to be a priest—by baptism or by consecration—you have to be able to laugh the gentle laugh, the kind that heals and holds and welcomes the Happy.

III.
Christ in Pigtails

Christ with me, Christ before me, Christ behind me,
Christ in me, Christ beneath me, Christ above me,
Christ on my right, Christ on my left,
Christ when I lie down, Christ when I sit down, Christ when I arise,
Christ in the heart of everyone who thinks of me,
Christ in the mouth of everyone who speaks of me,
Christ in every eye that sees me,
Christ in every ear that hears me.

The Breastplate of St. Patrick

Six-year-olds can be exasperating. They are whiny and hysterical little creatures that are more than willing to survive on a diet of macaroni and cheese, soft drinks, and Skittles. They glom and glower on the good days and can reduce the stalwart parent or nanny to dribbling gibberish on the bad. A six-year-old is not unlike the Chicago Cub fan, who has perfected over the decades a bemused detachment toward the Boys of Wrigley, captured perfectly by those crossed arms and those agnostic eyes that say in so many words, "Fool me once, shame on you. Fool me a hundred years in a row, shame on me." Cub fans and six-year-olds love you one moment and won't have anything to do with you the next.

Six-year-olds are also unrepentant danger-seekers. They don't think twice about lacing up the skates and gliding on thin ice and hoping for the best. It's all they know. Why would we expect otherwise? Most six-year-olds go to bed every night cognizant of the monsters that live in their closets or hunker patiently under their beds. Every morning comes as a reprieve, a temporary stay of execution. It makes sense that six-year-olds, knowing that the deck is stacked against them, would throw their whole selves into every day—laughing one moment and crying the next. It explains why they unscrew the training wheels from their bicycles months before they should. Hope beats eternal in their tiny little hearts, because they don't know any better.

Say what you will then about six-year-olds, but they are essentially truth-tellers. I remember hearing the story once of a mother who was trying to console her sobbing little girl upon the untimely demise of her pet cat Fluffy. The mother, thinking that granting the cat eternal life might placate her crestfallen child, comforted her daughter with words of hope.

Six-year-olds are we as we once were.

"Sweetheart," the mother said, "Try not to worry. Little Fluffy is with God in heaven now."

"But, Mommy," the little girl sniffled, "What does God want with a dead cat?"

Six-year-olds call it as they see it. They have yet to be introduced to the art of obfuscation or the bald-faced lie. It's worth it, putting up with the snot and croup and whining and woeful histrionics, knowing that your little boy or girl will tell you the truth, not because they necessarily want to but because they have to. I am sure that this was part of the reason Jesus pointed to little children and said that it was to the likes of them that the kingdom of God belonged. Children still believe that the truth really does set them free and that lies hammer nails into coffins. They are vulnerable and needy and hopeful little human beings that *cannot* tell a lie. They are we as we once were.

❊ ❊ ❊ ❊ ❊ ❊

Coming to the end of my seminary studies in preparation for ordained priestly ministry, I was intrigued by the faith of such children. I wanted to know how they appropriated the language, symbols, and rituals of faith. My hunch, confirmed by my research, was that children had a natural affinity to faith. However unpolished, unsophisticated, or unschooled it might be, their natural orientation was toward the divine. Part of my research involved interviewing first graders from one of the Catholic grade schools in the town of South Bend. I asked them all sorts of questions about their images of God, of heaven, and of Jesus. I had them draw me pictures of God, of themselves, and of their families, and with the help of a child psychologist at Notre Dame I did an analysis of those pictures. For me, though, all of the research and subsequent analysis was summarized by one interview I had with a six-year-old girl one afternoon. It was a moment of revelation, a divine encounter that I return to when my faith runs dry.

She came into the room wearing a beautiful white dress trimmed in lace. I surmised that she had just made her first holy communion. She wore little white socks and polished black shoes. Her short dark hair was bunched into pigtails. She sat in the chair with a shy smile and her hands folded neatly on her lap. Her legs, unable to reach the floor, swung back and forth. I went through the litany of questions that produced the six-year-old answers I had come to expect. It was my last interview of the day, and honestly I was a bit bored, so I asked the little girl a question I had not asked any of the others.

"Can you see God?" I asked.

The little girl's eyes opened wide and her smile grew large, as if she had been waiting her whole life for someone to ask her that very question.

"Oh, yes," she said.

I looked up, suddenly interested. "Is God here right now?" I asked her.

The little girl nodded.

"Where?" I asked.

The little girl gave me a look that said: *Are you an idiot? Can't you see?* She said in a whisper, "He's standing over here," and she pointed with her eyes to the right of her chair. "He's standing over here," and she pointed with her eyes to the left of her chair. Looking up she said, "He's above me." Looking under her chair and then at me she said, "He's below me." Finally, she said in the hushest of tones, "He's inside me."

❀ ❀ ❀ ❀ ❀ ❀ ❀

I have forty-nine years of life experience, more than five years of formal theological study, and over twenty years of life as a Holy Cross priest. Yet I am comforted by the words St. Thomas Aquinas was said to have uttered three months before he died: "All that I have written seems to me like straw compared with what has now been revealed to me." St. Thomas must have had an encounter similar to the one I had in South Bend years ago, when a little girl in pigtails let me know in no uncertain terms that God was alive and well and living in plain sight for everyone to see.

Six-year-olds are nettlesome little creatures who will drive most of us to distraction, but one thing we can count on: they will always tell us the truth.

SEVEN

Anointing of the Sick: A New Journey

Ahab told Jezebel all that Elijah had done,
and how he had killed all the prophets with the sword.
Then Jezebel sent a messenger to Elijah, saying,
"So may the gods do to me, and more also,
if I do not make your life like the life of one of them
by this time tomorrow."
Then Elijah was afraid; he got up and fled for his life,
and came to Beer-sheba, which belongs to Judah.
He left his servant there,
but he himself went a day's journey into the wilderness,
and came and sat down under a solitary broom tree.
He asked that he might die:
"It is enough; now, O LORD, take away my life,
for I am no better than my ancestors."
Then he lay down under the broom tree and fell asleep.
Suddenly an angel touched him and said to him,
"Get up and eat."
He looked, and there at his head
was a cake baked on hot stones, and a jug of water.
He ate and drank, and lay down again,
the angel of the LORD came a second time,
touched him, and said,
"Get up and eat, otherwise the journey will be too long for you."
He got up, and ate and drank;
then he went on the strength of that food
for forty days and forty nights to Horeb the mount of God.

1 Kings 19:1-8

I.
Holy Hands

On average, I got into a fistfight once a year when I was in grade school. Nicky Drabec, Pat Clancy, Richard Steinberg, Tim Quinn, Jim Pursiano. I remember them all. We used to fight at the statue of Our Lady of Grace behind the church so the nuns wouldn't catch us. Of course these major bouts did not include the scrapes I got into with my older brothers, with whom I fought on an almost daily basis at home. Looking back, I'm not surprised that the one prayer I remember my mother uttering more than any other was: "For Christ's sake, why can't you kids get along?"

I'm not sold on those theories presently being peddled by evolutionary biologists that seem to suggest that most of what we do as a species is genetically predetermined, but they do supply me with a ready answer to those who ask me how it is possible that I was such pugilist as a child, given my staunch pacifist leanings now.

It was my father.

My Uncle Bob, Dad's younger brother, loved to regale us with stories of those times when he, my dad, and their older brother Pat were in high school and how on most weekends in the fall they would head up to Klamath Falls in a pickup with a bunch of their pals and fight a few boys from the Klamath Union High School football team. They would return home bloodied and black-eyed and thoroughly happy. They were Irish-Catholic boys raised on the farm during the Great Depression by parents who did not suffer fools gladly and who, I now suspect, left their boys to themselves to find amusement where they could.

I look at old photographs of my dad when he was growing up and he always appeared with a wry smile on his face, as if he just got away with something. His high school pictures reveal a boy in a man's body: broad-chinned, a bemused look about him, arms crossed in subtle defiance. He looked like the kind of kid I wouldn't have minded hanging out with when I was in high school. He could get into his fair share of trouble, but come Sunday, having been duly shriven on Saturday afternoon, he took communion on the tongue.

The fruit does not fall far from the tree. I remember one summer afternoon getting into a tussle with my brother Jack, four years my senior. I was eight or nine. The argument escalated and Jack became quite agitated with me. Figuring I was going to get a pretty good hiding if I stuck to the confines of our home, I bolted out of the house and ran out into the street. Jack took chase. I ran all the way down Arcadian Drive, passing one gawking neighbor after another who were enjoying the spectacle of a boy trying desperately to outrun his older brother while screaming like a banshee. I ran for a quarter of a mile before collapsing on some stranger's lawn. My brother arrived forthwith and pummeled me.

We served at Mass together that next Sunday.

❋ ❋ ❋ ❋ ❋ ❋ ❋

My fighting instinct was my father's blood coursing in my veins. He never took me aside and taught me how to use my fists. I rarely heard him raise his voice and never saw him fight. Even now the prevailing image of my father is of a slightly overweight, middle-aged man in a suit and loosened tie with black-rimmed glasses on the edge of his nose sipping on a whiskey and water while watching Walter Cronkite on the television. As a kid I used to sit on his lap on such evenings and press my hands against his and study them thoroughly: the nicks and cuts, the calluses and scars. I realized that, yes, under a very thin suburban veneer, my dad was a true fighter.

By the time I got to know him, he was a lawyer, and by everyone's account a darn good one. He was the attorney you went to when you were the underdog. He must have traded in his boxing gloves for the blistering cross-examination and found the latter more satisfying. As I grew older it became obvious that I was my father's son, two males who blended fist and faith and found no unsettling contradiction in their commingling.

Dad and I shared the same name; we were both southpaws. Heck, we even had the same blood type. For most—if not all—of my life, then, I never feared my father; but I was in awe of him. I knew he had a temper as fiery as my own, but he seemed to use it as fuel for higher purposes: for defending vulnerable folk, for lifting people up when no one else would, for fighting the good fight. I loved him for that.

❈ ❈ ❈ ❈ ❈ ❈ ❈

I recall the night my brother Jack called to tell me that Dad had died suddenly from a heart attack. I went back to my room in the seminary and lay on my bed. Memories poured out as balm to soothe the open wound, and none soothed me more than the memory of what might have been the last fistfight my father ever had. I was not a witness to the event, but Uncle Bob loved to tell of it, free of selfish slant or unnecessary exaggeration.

No memory soothed me more

than the memory

of what might have been

the last fistfight

my father ever had.

One Saturday night Uncle Bob and Aunt Barbara were at our house for dinner. They were in their mid-thirties at the time, Dad and Uncle Bob, brothers and both attorneys in town and family men with thirteen children between the two of them. By evening's end they were both a bit silly from the drink and subsequently regressed to their adolescent pattern of ragging on each other. Uncle Bob let slip some unflattering observation of my dad's wife, our mother. Dad took immediate umbrage and told Uncle Bob to apologize. Uncle Bob refused.

"Your dad looked at me and started to smile," Uncle Bob said. "I knew I was a dead man."

Dad and Uncle Bob proceeded to fight right there in the living room, and Dad was having the better of it. Mom was begging her husband to stop, and when that didn't work she woke up the oldest of her brood, Brian. "Stop your father," she said. "He's going to kill Uncle Bob!" Brian, nine years old, ran out of the bedroom and jumped onto Dad's back, yelling at him to stop, which he finally did.

The best part of the story is this: the next day was the Super Bowl. Uncle Bob showed up the next morning for the game. He and Dad sat together on the couch and watched the game as if nothing had happened. After all, they were brothers. Brothers fight, but brothers forgive and love one another.

I lay on my bed that night of Dad's death and drew satisfaction from that story, because it defined my father for me. He was a good and imperfect man, a man of unimpeachable integrity and subtle passion. He taught me in a hundred ways how to negotiate my way through the world. He taught me how to make the sign of the cross with hands that could, when provoked by bullies or brothers, make a fist. He taught me how to be a good brother and brother-in-law and uncle and priest.

❊ ❊ ❊ ❊ ❊ ❊

Years later I was by the hospital bed of my Uncle Bob. He had been struck down by encephalitis and was in dire straits. He could barely speak. I asked if he wanted to be anointed, and he nodded. As I prayed over him and with him, I anointed Bob's forehead. Then I took his hands to anoint them, as is the Catholic custom. They were callused, weatherworn, farming hands to the end, and they looked just like my dad's. I marveled at the stories those hands might have told: of holding beautiful women in moonlight and caressing the cheek of the one who would be his wife, of handshakes that sealed deals and forged friendships, of combat with friend and foe and family alike.

Before I left I kissed Uncle Bob on the forehead and told him I loved him, words I did not have the opportunity to tell my father before he died. In barely audible words, Bob told me he loved me too, and I knew he was speaking for Dad as well. It brought me great solace to know that when Bob arrived in heaven my father would be there to welcome him with open arms and hands outstretched and that neither of them would ever form a fist again. Their hands were anointed, after all, fit now only for loving.

II.
The Playground

There is a park in my hometown where I used to spend many of my summer days as a child along with my brothers and sisters and kids from the neighborhood. It had everything a child would want in a park: a snack bar, a baseball diamond, basketball courts, swings and monkey bars, and a bucolic field enshadowed by huge, climbable oak trees for picnicking. The most popular feature of the park, however, was the winged fuselage of an old World War II-era airplane, which sat in a sand box adjacent to the swings. Bare feet burned on the sun-percolated steel of that old plane, but none of us cared. Slipping into its cockpit was too irresistible for our ripe imaginations.

On any given summer day the Community Center, as we called it, would be overrun by kids. While young moms and dads kept a hawk eye on their toddlers, the rest of us policed ourselves, relying upon an unwritten code of juvenile conduct, which for the most part kept us from brawling. There was a canine quality to our interactions. We mostly moved in packs, gave grudging respect to the older kids, maintained a skeptical stance towards strangers, and mostly frolicked, as dogs are wont to do when loosed from the leash.

❊ ❊ ❊ ❊ ❊ ❊ ❊

It was dusk, and the park was near empty that early fall evening. The coastal fog had rolled in and cast everything in an eerie gray. I was sitting in the cockpit of that old warplane lost in a narrative pieced and spliced together from a hundred war movies. *We're losing power, Mac!* I said—or something like it—to my invisible co-pilot. *I can't shake the Japs, Mac. They're coming at us at three-o'clock! Rat-a-tat, rat-a-tat!* And so on. My nerves of steel and Zen-like calm gave Mac courage as we faced down the enemy together. *When we get back to the base, Mac, the first round is on me.* I smile at my imaginary friend, who in the movie in my mind is just a kid out of high school. It makes me feel good to know that he trusts me, his superior officer. I can't let anything happen to him. He's got a girl back home.

Directly in front of me, I see them coming: four teenaged boys. As they pass the monkey bars they notice me in the cockpit and stop. Something did not feel right. I didn't know who they were, kids from another part of town I guessed. One of them was smoking a cigarette.

"Hey, punk," one of them said as they neared the plane, "come down here. We want to talk to you." They bore cold smiles.

"That's okay," I said in a high-pitched voice. My heart was beating furiously as I looked around to see if there was anyone else in the park who might come to my aid. I was alone. The older boys surrounded the plane like jackals around a wayward and wounded pup.

"You come down, or we come up," another said. They weren't smiling anymore. I was frantic. I could start screaming, but in my seven-year-old mind I quickly dismissed that option, as this would demoralize Mac, who was still sitting next to me. I needed to be brave for both of us.

I slowly climbed out of the cockpit and made my way to the cold sand where immediately the four boys surrounded me.

"What do you think we should do to him?" one of them said. Honest to God, I was five seconds from wetting my pants. The one smoking a cigarette stepped forward and looked at me straight in the eye. He took a long drag from his cigarette and then, holding it over my crew-cut head, tapped it a few times. A long trail of ash fell onto my head and as it began to burn, they laughed at me, a human ashtray.

"I don't think you want to do that again." Thirty feet away an even older kid, maybe eighteen, stood. Where he had come from I had no clue, but there he was, and by the tone of his voice you knew he meant business. He began to walk toward us, and the four miscreants looked at each other and, having sized up the situation, decided to slowly slink away.

The stranger came up to me, and I stood there mute before him. Brushing the ashes off of my head, he asked, "Are you okay, kid?"

"Yes," I said with my high-pitched, still-petrified voice.

"Why don't you head back home," he said.

"Okay," I said, obediently, and I began my mile-long trek back to Arcadian Drive with Mac, who was incredibly gracious by not saying a word to anyone about what had happened.

❈ ❈ ❈ ❈ ❈ ❈ ❈

It was autumn of 1997 and recess time at St. Felicitas School in San Leandro, California, where I was serving as an associate pastor. Jump rope and hopscotch occupied the northwest corner. A rather intense game of dodge ball was unfolding on the patch of asphalt closest to the church. A gaggle of eighth-grade girls sat at the picnic tables nestled in the shade. Occasionally one screamed and ran into the bathroom with two or three in hot pursuit. First graders and kindergartners were entertaining the two or three teachers on patrol with their handstands and cartwheels. It was a snapshot of peaceful civility. This was what we all hope for the world: no borders; no boundaries, no divisions.

On a bench in a hidden corner, however, I spied a little boy all by himself, eating a bologna sandwich.

From a distance,
he appeared perfectly content,
like a monk at home
in his cell of solitude.
But it did appear
oddly out of place.

His blue trousers were perfectly pressed; his white polo shirt was neatly tucked in. He sipped his milk carefully. Not a crumb of his sandwich fell to the ground. His legs, which did not quite reach the ground, swung to and fro to the beat of some invisible drum. From a distance, he appeared perfectly content, like a monk at home in his cell of solitude. But it did appear oddly out of place that one so young would choose such solitary confinement over the company of his mates, and so I made my way over to the bench where this young boy sat alone. When I was maybe ten feet away, the true story began to unfold.

His eyes stared at the ground. He seemed to be chewing but I don't think he was swallowing. My shadow reached him before I did, and he must have sensed my presence. He took one last sip from his milk before he looked up. He was not smiling. A deep sadness rested in his eyes, and I was sure that the moment I uttered a word he would start crying.

"Hello, Jimmy!" I said, walking over to him. "How are you doing?"

Sure enough, Jimmy's lower lip began to quiver, and tears streamed from his eyes. The beginnings of worry lines around his eyes appeared. He was growing old before my eyes. I sat right next to him and put my arm around his shaking shoulders. Thank God no one could see him. Shame would only have compounded his misery.

"No one wants to play with me, Father," Jimmy finally confessed, and it was uttered like a death sentence, which no doubt is how it must have been handed down to him by his Christian comrades: a little second grader cast aside like a pair of worn-out sneakers. Jimmy had been left to fend for himself in shadow and shade. What sin had this child commited to warrant such action? Had he stolen someone's lunch money? Had he kicked a puppy or tied soda pop cans to the tail of a kitten? I gently probed, but the convict did not quickly confess his crime, so heavy the burden of shame he carried. So I just sat there with him, content to pass the rest of recess with the little criminal.

"I wet my pants," Jimmy suddenly blurted out. (Oh, my goodness, I thought. Now I've done it! I'd rattled the poor kid so much that I made him pee right then and there! What kind of a dumb priest am I!) As Jimmy looked up at me, I looked down at him. His blue trousers were perfectly dry. "I wet my pants yesterday, Father Pat. It was an accident, but now no one wants to be my friend."

I sat with the little boy for a few more minutes and let him wipe his tears with my handkerchief. I told him everything would be okay. But I wasn't so sure it would. Kids can be pretty mean and unforgiving when they want to. I remember many times from my own childhood when I was held in my misery by others. I also remember holding others in theirs.

That day, I did my priestly best to discreetly notify the principal about Jimmy's siutation, and I'm sure she handled It. But I had enough of my own childhood traumas to recognize that they do hurt, sometimes for a lifetime.

❀ ❀ ❀ ❀ ❀ ❀

Every now and then I think of Jimmy and the look of devastation on his face. He must be nineteen now. I think of the encounter Jesus had with a woman whose frail and broken humanity—like Jimmy's—had also been exposed for the whole world to see, a woman who had been caught in the sin of adultery. The Mosaic Law required that she be taken out and hammered with rocks and stones until she was dead.

Jesus simply invited those around him to see themselves in this woman and admit that none of them would leave the planet without sin, without getting at least a little dirty, without wetting their pants once or twice.

At the end of that story, all that remained were Jesus and the woman, or as St. Augustine famously saw it, "There were but two left: misery and mercy." And in the end, we know how the story ends. Even misery departs; mercy stands alone.

Maybe that is what we are all supposed to do when facing the misery of others: stand next to them mercifully as they die just a little and tell them in so many words that everything will be okay, even if we are not so sure.

III.
Big Mac Sauce and
Other Lessons on Love

One thing you discover upon starting to work at any McDonald's restaurant is that you can never really get rid of the aroma of their "special sauce." The mixture of mayonnaise and pickles and God-only-knows-what-else that gives the Big Mac sandwich its unique taste has a way of insinuating itself into the fabric of your clothing and will outlast the best efforts of any washing machine. I would scrub myself down every night after work with the fervor of one who had been exposed to uranium, only to find classmates the next day in the hallway sniffing the air as I passed by. After a few weeks, however, you never really notice the smell anymore. It becomes part of the landscape, like a light coating of dust on the living room furniture or those human foibles and habits that in time serve only to amuse and entertain.

I suppose it may seem odd that it is this indelible aroma that first comes to mind when I recall my days of sweat and toil at the McDonald's on Strobridge Avenue in my hometown. It is a memory I can still taste, still smell. It draws me back to a group of people I once knew, men and women and teenaged boys and girls who grilled burgers and tended to the deep fryers and worked the cash registers and wiped down tables. It was a crossroads of intersecting lives heading off in a hundred directions: those of my ilk, saving money for college; high school drop-outs, earning beer and rent money; a succession of transients, stopping briefly in our town before moving on to another; balding men and hair-dyed women, holding on for dear life and the modicum of dignity that only a regular paycheck can bring. When we met at the crossroads—the time clock at Mickey D's that punched us in and out—no one was greater or lesser than anyone else. We *all* smelled like special sauce.

✺ ✺ ✺ ✺ ✺ ✺

The smell of that sauce also reminds me of the regular customers, usually older men and sometimes their spouses, who arrived punctually every day for their daily sustenance. It reminds me especially of one couple, Fred and Lois.

I was working the grill the day Fred and Lois first came in. Their dark green Dodge pulled into the parking spot closest to the trash compactor, and Fred got out first and hustled over to the other side of the car to open the door for Lois. She took his outstretched hand, and together they made their way to the restaurant. They ordered two Quarter Pounders with Cheese (with catsup only), two orders of small fries, and two black coffees. When one of my co-workers, Peggy, passed the grill slip back to me, we exchanged sheepish grins, because we both had already fallen hopelessly in love with Fred and Lois.

They were no taller than five feet, both of them, two peas from the same tiny pod. He was in a worn but tidy wool suit with a fat tie from the forties that hung well above his belt buckle. She wore a simple yet stylish dress that reminded me of something June Cleaver would have worn on *Leave It to Beaver*—if the Cleaver family had ever gone out to dinner at a fast-food restaurant. The couple were in their seventies as best we could tell, but they looked like newlyweds. Maybe it was the way they stood at the counter: one body ever so slightly leaning into the other, helplessly reacting to the divine gravitational pull that insisted that their bodies should be one. Maybe it was the way Lois doted on Fred, patting her lace handkerchief on his sweated brow. Maybe it was the way he *let* her dote on him. But I remember thinking, even at my young age at the time, that they made a lovely couple sitting in the booth at McDonald's at four-thirty every afternoon, eating their burgers cooked to order, munching on their fries, sipping their coffee, and casting gazes upon each other like they were still in high school.

Fred and Lois arrived every afternoon at the same time, Monday through Friday, and ordered the same meal. It got so we anticipated their arrival. As their car pulled up, someone would sound the alarm and we would quickly get to work making their burgers exactly how they liked them. We made sure the fries were piping hot and crisp and the coffee steaming; and when Fred and Lois walked into the restaurant, their meal would be waiting for them every time, and as they shuffled to their booth the rest of us would smile at each other, grateful for the small role we were playing in this quiet drama of grace and beauty.

One day they didn't come in. Then a week passed, and then another. There was still no Fred and Lois. Maybe they were on vacation, one of us said. Yeah, that's what's happened. They're visiting the grandkids. Secretly though, we all harbored the thought that something awful had happened. Every day at four-thirty we waited for the green Dodge to pull into the parking lot. But it never came.

We could tell by the way his shoulders drooped that Lois would not be joining him for dinner that night, or ever again.

Several months passed. And then one day, at four-thirty, one of us spotted the Dodge making the turn into the lot. A cheer rang out in the restaurant as our worst fears dissolved in a sea of euphoria. We were giddy with excitement as we prepared their two Quarter Pounder Extra Value Meals with coffee. We added two chocolate sundaes no charge because we were, quite frankly, relieved at seeing them again.

But Fred walked in alone. We could tell by the way his shoulders drooped that Lois would not be joining him for dinner that night, or ever again. He approached the counter before Peggy could hide the tray and took notice of the meal prepared for two. His eyes began to well up, and tears came to every one of our eyes too. Peggy came from behind the counter and hugged him, and all of us teenagers huddled around him him because we couldn't think of what else to do.

✾ ✾ ✾ ✾ ✾ ✾

I worked at McDonald's over thirty years ago. I am sure Fred has joined Lois by now. All of us who met at that crossroads have moved on, unless Peggy is still working there. Of those days I am left now with only a few memories, like the one of Fred and Lois walking up to the counter and seeing their meals waiting for them. But another memory that I cannot shake is of a bunch of teenagers huddled around Fred when he came back to us all by himself. Try as I might, there are some things I simply can never get rid of. I wouldn't want to, because they reveal to me the face of God.

Blood Brothers

He was smaller than I was. I remember that, but I do not recall his name. I remember it was in the summer of my fifth year. I was going to be attending Clifton School's kindergarten class in the fall, and toward the end of summer I took periodic walks by myself from my home on Arcadian Drive to Clifton, committing the twenty-minute journey to muscle memory so I would not lose my way when the first day of classes began.

On one of those walks I met him for the first time. I observe now how five-year-olds relate to others, and I am always stunned by the ease with which they enter into conversation. They are unencumbered, free of the self-conscious ghost that haunts and coaxes many of us into a sheepish, shy, and awkward posture. Five-year-olds will talk with anyone, even another five-year-old who is a perfect stranger.

If you had passed by us that day near Clifton School, you would have seen two boys sitting under a tree talking to each other intently, like old men on a park bench. We had first observed each other on opposite sides of a chain-linked fence. Both of us were blue-jeaned and tee-shirted, with hair matted down from dirt and summer sweat. I had never met him before, but there he was in his front yard looking at me.

"Hey," one of us must have said.

"Hey," the other must have responded. That's how it was done then.

He was a Protestant, and I was a Catholic. He asked me straight off.

"What religion are you?" he asked.

"Catholic," I said. "You?"

"Christian," he said.

"Oh," I probably said.

I remember that we established our religious pedigrees right away, because our conversation eventually turned on our understanding of heaven and hell and who went where. It isn't all that unusual for children to ask such personal questions. I remember once being at the city pool and seeing a man sitting at the edge with only one leg. The other was a mere stub. I swam over to him and stood there in the water for a moment looking at his amputated limb.

"What happened to your leg?" I asked.

"Oh, a crocodile bit it off," he said, and I thought that was both sad and incredibly interesting.

"Can I touch it?" I asked.

"No," he said, and that was that.

❄ ❄ ❄ ❄ ❄ ❄ ❄

I stood there on one side of the fence while the boy I had met stood on the other side. After a while we must have decided to walk across the street where a huge oak tree stood. There we sat and conversed in the shade.

I was vaguely aware that there were other folks in town who were not Catholic.

He was unusually interested in my religion. Apparently he had been told that Catholics were going to hell, and now that he had a real live Catholic in front of him he wanted to explore the issue, at a five-year-old level, of course. I had grown up thinking that Catholics had as good a shot—maybe even the best shot—at getting into heaven as anyone else. I was vaguely aware of the fact that there were other folks in town who were not Catholic, but it never seemed to bother me. But this boy, all of five, already had a finely etched image of salvation that pointedly did not include Catholics.

I did the best I could defending my faith. I was still two years away from receiving my First Holy Communion, but with a year or two of informal lessons from my parents and siblings on the subject, I felt confident enough to speak with relative authority on why I already believed that Holy Communion would insure my salvation.

For as long as I could remember (which, as I think of it, wasn't that

long at all), I had wanted to go to communion. I sat impatiently week after week in the pew on Sunday as my mother and father and older brothers and sisters climbed over my bony legs and joined that long line to the
communion rail, where Fr. Stack would feed them the Bread of Life. I sat
there with my book of the saints, and read and reread the story of the
boy-saint who fell upon ruffians on the way to bringing Holy Communion to the homebound and died rather than hand over the consecrated
hosts tucked away safely near his heart.

I told the Protestant boy that we Catholics ate the Body of Christ and
that this was "food for the journey" as my mother would say often when
I was growing up. (Later, when she was near death and I had given her
communion for the last time, she said it again.)

I told the boy I believed in Jesus and had been baptized when I was
just a day old, a fact he found fascinating. I told him everything I knew
about my faith, little truths I had discerned by looking around the church
during Mass or listening to my family's conversation around the dinner
table. I told him about older kids and men and women going into a dark
box of a room and confessing sins to a priest, whom I already knew was
Christ in forgiving flesh. I told him about the gold tabernacle where the
priest put Jesus after communion. I told him about holy water that you
blessed yourself with. I told him about the sign of the cross.

"Sign of the cross?" he said. "What's that?"

I made the sign of the cross and showed him how to do it and what
to say. Looking back, I guess was giving him permission to touch *my*
severed limb. I was letting him into the deepest part of my life, shrouded
as it is in mystery and majesty and suffering and joy. He followed my lead
and made the sign of the cross for the first time. It did not seem to have
any discernable effect on him that day. Soon after I said I had to go and
I did.

❀ ❀ ❀ ❀ ❀ ❀ ❀

A week or so later I bumped into the same kid again. He was on one
side of the fence, and I was on the other side.

"Hey," one of us must have said.

"Hey," the other must have responded.

"Would you be my blood brother?" he asked me.

"Okay," I said, not knowing at all what that meant.

We walked over to a secluded corner of the school across the street. He took out a Swiss army knife, retrieved one of the blades, and told me to hold out my finger, which I did. First he nicked his own finger, drawing an immediate bubble of thick red blood to the skin surface. Then he reached over, took my hand, and gently nicked my finger. I remember thinking that we were sharing something special, that this must have had something to do with our previous conversation. When my fingertip was sufficiently bloody, the boy took his finger and pressed it against mine and kept it there for a moment.

"There," he said, "now we're blood brothers forever."

For the next year or so we would occasionally cross paths as I walked to and from Clifton School. He would say "Hey," and I would say "Hey." And then we would both say, in unison, "Blood brothers!"

To this day I am convinced that this was this boy's way of telling me that he had changed his mind about Catholics going to hell or, at the very least, that he had made an exception in my case. I think it was his way of saying that we were both going to get into heaven somehow.

This story, and this book, has God's fingerprints all over it, because God and all human beings are blood brothers and sisters ever since Jesus mixed his blood with ours on the Cross. That mystery was, and continues to be, humanity's long yearning's end.